**FAST FORWARD: The New
Television and American Society**

The New Television and American Society

Essays from *Channels of Communications*

Edited by

Les Brown and Savannah Waring Walker

ANDREWS AND MCMEEL, INC.
A Universal Press Syndicate Company
Kansas City • New York

Library of Congress Cataloging in Publication Data
Main entry under title:

Fast forward.

    1. Television broadcasting—Social aspects—United States—Addresses, essays, lectures. 2. Television industry—United States—Addresses, essays, lectures. 3. Television broadcasting of news—United States—Addresses, essays, lectures. I. Brown, Les, 1928-
II. Walker, Savannah Waring, 1957-
PN1992.6.F3   1983   791.45'0973   83-6033
ISBN 0-8362-6208-5

Contents

Contributors

JONATHAN BLACK is an editor at *TV-Cable Week* magazine and a frequent contributor to *Channels*.

LES BROWN is editor-in-chief of *Channels* and former television editor for *The New York Times* and *Variety*.

DAVID BURNHAM is a *New York Times* reporter and author of *The Rise of the Computer State* (Random House).

ROBERT COLES is a child psychiatrist at the Harvard University Health Services. He is author of *Children of Crisis* and winner of the Four Freedoms Award and the Pulitzer Prize.

WILLIAM A. HENRY III who writes national news for *Time* magazine, received the 1980 Pulitzer Prize for criticism as television critic of *The Boston Globe*.

WALTER KARP is a political writer whose latest book is *The Politics of War* (Harper & Row).

MARTIN KOUGHAN is a CBS News producer and a frequent contributor to *Channels*.

CHARLES KURALT is a CBS News correspondent and anchorman for CBS's "Sunday Morning."

CHRISTOPHER LASCH, professor of history at the University of Rochester, is author of *The Culture of Narcissism.*

STEVEN LEVY writes frequently for *Esquire, Rolling Stone,* and other publications.

MICHAEL MALONE writes for *The New York Times Book Review* and is the author of several books, including *Dingley Falls* (Harcourt Brace Jovanovich).

HORACE NEWCOMB, an associate professor of English at the Austin campus of the University of Texas, is the author of *TV: The Most Popular Art,* and editor of *Television: The Critical View.*

EDWIN NEWMAN is an NBC News correspondent and author of *A Civil Tongue.*

MICHAEL POLLAN is senior editor of *Channels.*

WILLIAM H. PRITCHARD teaches English at Amherst College and is author of *The Lives of the Modern Poets.*

SYLVIA RABINER is a New York writer and teacher.

HERBERT SCHILLER, professor of communications at the University of California, San Diego, is the author of *Who Knows: Information in the Age of the Fortune 500* (Ablex).

RALPH LEE SMITH is director of policy and planning studies for the Bertman Group, a telecommunications consulting firm.

JULIE TALEN is a reporter for *Television Digest* and a frequent contributor to *Channels.*

MEL WATKINS is an editor at *The New York Times Book Review.* He is currently writing a book on black-American humor.

CLARK WHELTON, speechwriter for the mayor of New York, is writing a book on television.

BRIAN WINSTON is a professor of film and television at New York University.

MICHAEL WOOD is a professor of English at Exeter University. He is the author of *America in the Movies* and of a forthcoming book on Luis Buñuel.

FAST FORWARD: The New Television and American Society

Introduction

No technology of the twentieth century has inspired a deeper ambivalence in us than television. At times we're grateful for its ball games, royal weddings, election returns, and pleasant weekly series; at others, we resent that it holds half the nation in its thrall night after night with scant intellectual nourishment and that it injects itself into the processes of politics, sports, religion, education, and even diplomacy. Even after a third of a century we haven't yet, as a society, made peace with the idea of broadcast television, or made up our minds whether on balance it is a positive or negative force in our midst. And now, in a rush, comes the New Television to complicate the issue and change yet again how we live.

The New Television is the future we used to speak of a few years ago, arrived. It combines an explosion of channels with a rash of new communications systems: two-way cable, videotex, interactive video discs, satellite-to-home broadcasting, pay-per-view television, videoconferencing, video games, and electronic mail. A whole new electronic landscape has grown up around us, made up of microwaves, laser beams, microprocessors, and electronic pulses moving along wires leading to display on the television screen.

This new age is on fast forward, shaking the foundations of conventional television and sweeping over all our social institu-

1

tions as if determined to transform the world by 1990. It is a phenomenon born of two monumental developments: the running together of four previously discrete technologies—cable, computers, satellites, and telephone—that combine to produce remarkable delivery systems; and the discovery, which came in the late seventies, that people are actually willing to pay for certain kinds of television, principally movies, uncut and without commercials.

Paying for television changes everything—the economy that shaped commercial television and the competitive structure of the marketplace. Obviously people will watch what they pay for, and it follows that as the number of paying customers grows, the Nielsen numbers for conventional television will decline. Already the networks' share of the audience has eroded significantly.

What also changes are people's attitudes toward television. If we put our own money down, by our own choice, we can no longer disdain the medium or speak of it as "the idiot box." Thus television, in the new age, gains a more respectful audience and becomes a subject safe again for intelligent discussion. A benign effect of cable's marriage to computers and satellites is that television may belong once more to people who read. And an audience of readers makes possible a new kind of television criticism.

Television fell out of favor with the intelligentsia in America somewhere around the time Milton Berle's broad comedy became the national sensation on Tuesday nights. Before Berle's "Texaco Star Theatre," television was a luxury enjoyed mainly by affluent families, whose tastes were catered to, a good part of the time, with live studio drama. Television was emerging as an electronic theater then and seemed on its way to fostering an important literature of its own. Berle, however, made television popular in working-class households, and when it became the medium for the masses, its programming shot off on a new course. With that, the character and direction of television criticism also changed.

For television's great popularity and pervasiveness made it a threat to all printed media; it competed not only for the consumer's time but for the advertising the print media depended on. When general-interest magazines and local newspapers began folding in the late fifties, publishers contrived a strategy to fight the electronic menace. It was a strategy of derision: Make people ashamed of watching television. It worked, especially with the intelligentsia.

From that point, most of the serious writing about television was by design essentially hostile to the medium and full of ominous, sometimes hysterical, speculation about its poisonous influence on children and the moral fabric of the society. Television was berated systematically in the press for its commercial excesses and the inanity of its popular programs; it was hooted at as "the boob tube" and "chewing gum for the eyes," undeserving of any thinking person's attention. Some thirty years later, throughout many of the print media, the tradition continues. Newspapers that would not dream of appointing a literary critic who did not love books, or a drama critic who did not revere the theater, still look for the kind of television critic who dependably will not give comfort to the enemy. No experience necessary.

These days, when the writing is not overtly derisive, it minimizes television another way, by underscoring the medium's triviality in heavy concentrations of celebrity interviews and industry gossip. A newspaper editor once explained to me why he found it pointless to attempt any substantive examination of television. "This is a shallow medium for shallow people," he said blandly. "If we tried to write seriously about it, who would read it? Not the intellectuals, because they're not interested in television. And not the people who really care about television, because all they ever want to know from us is what's on tonight."

Of course, a good many journalists writing about television today do perform their work earnestly and labor in hopes of establishing some legitimacy for their field. But they are up against something even more frustrating than the biases of editors, for they are dealing with a medium virtually immune to criticism. In other areas of the arts, the judgment of reviewers often governs success or failure; but television reviewers have almost no power over the hits and flops in prime time. This reflects not on their credibility but on the medium's incredible scale. Television's audience is so large that the portion of it actually heeding a reviewer's advice is almost negligible when translated into a Nielsen rating.

A book that sells 30,000 copies thanks to the praise of critics is a hit; a play that is SRO for a season in a 1,000-seat house is a smash. But a television show with a prime-time audience of 20 million viewers is a failure, even though that single night's audience is sufficient to fill a fair-sized Broadway theater to capacity every performance, for forty years.

Moreover, television doesn't need reviews, as the other art forms do, to help it amass an audience. Television generates its own audience just by being television. People watch in predictable numbers every time period of the week, regardless of what is being shown.

What kind of criticism is indicated, then, for this colossus of popular culture, which wipes aside the judgments of the most powerful newspapers and magazines and heeds only the voice of the Nielsen opinion polls? Can anything ever be written or said about television that would make the merest difference in what it presents and how it performs? Does it suffice for criticism to provide a reader's service every day offering guidance on what to watch?

These are questions left over from the first age of television. The new age, with all its promise and portents of change, raises questions of its own.

The promise, the portents, and the questions were, in fact, what led to the creation of the magazine, *Channels of Communications,* in the spring of 1981. *Channels* set out to advance a new kind of television criticism, one devoid of the old antitelevision cant, that would not make judgments on individual programs but rather would seek to make meaning of television. At the same time, it aimed to interpret for a general readership the developments in the emerging new electronic age and the social issues rising from them. The magazine has developed as one for people interested in public affairs, who recognize that television is nothing less than the most potent social, political, and cultural force in our time.

This book, which represents some of the exemplary writing in *Channels,* introduces both the components of the new age and the essence of the new criticism. The ruling technologies do not spring from any cosmic planning by our government but are rooted in business. Therefore, part of the nation will be wired for cable, while the other part is to be served by direct-broadcast satellites. Government is striving to create an open marketplace in which all the new media may compete, in the apparent hope that the activity will revitalize the economy and point the way to the reindustrialization of America.

It is important to know, then, that the imperatives of business determine what is possible, most of the time, and that it is quite futile to think of television—in either the old or new form—in utopian terms. On the other hand, it is sheer lunacy to allow business to have its own way. If its quests should threaten our personal rights and freedoms, or our country's relations with foreign nations, that's where the work of the new television journalism begins. The more government recedes from the picture, the greater the need for incisive reporting to safeguard the public's stake in the new video age.

As for the new criticism, it accepts the fact that the Nielsens rule commercial television and posits that popularity is itself worthy of examination, because of what it reveals about ourselves as a people at a moment in time. If this criticism will not avail, under our system, to make expert judgments on the artistic merits of any program, then it is wise to consider instead why programs do catch on and what they tell us about our national psyche. Television was never so much our window on the world as our mirror on ourselves.

This kind of television criticism follows the lead of literary criticism in the twentieth century, which has become less concerned with judging a work for its beauty than with understanding it. In television, the issue is not what statement a single program might make, since it is likely to have been manufactured by a committee under the guidance of a network ratings strategist, but what statement a whole television season makes. Of course, it remains necessary to prod the medium to improve journalistically and artistically, but some methods of prodding are oblique, and thus perhaps more effective overall.

A power greater than the colossus of television is the power of public opinion—which begins with knowing. The power of the press is not in the printed word but in the reader. This book is for readers.

Les Brown

1.

Birth of a Wired Nation

Ralph Lee Smith

*I*n *May 1970, Ralph Lee Smith's article in* The Nation *attracted wide interest for its assertion that the United States would soon be substantially wired from coast to coast for cable television. Entitled "The Wired Nation," the article not only covered the social potential of the intriguing new medium but also the policy questions it raised. In 1972, an expanded version of the article was published as a book by Harper & Row. However, when cable faltered in its first attempts to penetrate the major cities, its glamor evaporated, and Smith's prediction was dismissed like an erroneous weather forecast.*

Now the picture has changed. Cable has begun to spread rapidly across the country, as was predicted a decade ago. Here, Smith takes a fresh look at cable, assesses its development, and reexamines his earlier conclusions.

The future arrived officially on the eighteenth of May, 1980, the day the National Cable Television Association convention opened in Dallas. History was not so much made at this event as marked by it. Scores of people not directly involved in the cable industry—financiers, corporation executives, producers, city government officials, and journalists—were drawn to the convention by a powerful sense that something momentous was happening in America. Whether or not they thought about it in these terms, they had made their pilgrimage to Dallas to witness the birth of the New Age of Television.

It was clear that America was on the threshold of becoming a "wired nation," that in the next few years homes and offices all across the country would be equipped for cable television, the rapidly expanding technology that creates dozens of new channels in each community, foreseeably as many as, or more than, fifty.

Old ideas about broadcasting for mass audiences are rendered obsolete by this profusion of television channels. They can potentially break the lock-step of existing commercial television; they can bring a greater variety of informational, educational, and cultural viewing material to the home screen, and can serve the needs of communities, smaller audiences, and special groups. They lend themselves also to new forms of communications services, such as the transmission of textual material, pay television, and home security systems. Cable promises, at once, a television renaissance and tantalizing opportunities for new wealth.

The new networks, pay services, and technical devices introduced at the Dallas convention all reflected the robustness of the industry and signified that cable was now truly, after several tentative starts, on the move across the land. The communications revolution that began incongruously in rural areas and small towns was expanding its programming store as it was beginning to sweep the cities. During the next three or four years most major metropolitan markets will be franchised for cable. Well before the end of this decade the United States will be a wired nation. And when this wiring is done, things will never be quite the same again.

It must be said, however, that costs prohibit the country's ever becoming *completely* wired. Large geographical areas—the sparsely settled countryside between urban centers—will probably never have cable because the cost of "laying hard wire" is so great that no company could find it profitable to build systems there. The American Broadcasting Companies Inc. was probably correct when it estimated, in 1975 testimony before a Senate subcommittee, that the cost of wiring half the country would be $10 billion—and the cost for the other half $250 billion.

The portions of the country not covered by cable are likely to be served instead by satellites broadcasting directly to homes, and by the newly authorized low-power television stations. One way or another, these areas will also experience an explosion of channels, and will thus share in the bounty of the wired nation.

A wired nation holds out the promise of convenience, entertainment in abundance, and many other remarkable new uses for the cathode ray tube; it does not, however, promise utopia. For all its allure, the phenomenon is fraught with serious policy questions. Many were raised a decade ago when cable seemed about to embrace the cities, but they remain unresolved and as complex today as they were in 1970. In this decade, we can neither ignore the questions nor delay difficult decisions. If cable is to serve our nation well, we must now look for answers to questions like these:

Who will control these powerful new communications systems, and how much should government regulate them? Who will have access rights to cable and how should that be used? What material should be allowed into American homes? Is it healthy for the parties who control the program sources to operate the cable systems through which they are delivered?

Should telephone companies be allowed to operate cable systems and thereby deliver both telephone and television over a single wire? If so, should the federal government regulate—or should the municipality? What should the new rules be? Finally, as companies frantically scramble for cable franchises in the large cities, are they promising more than they can possibly deliver? And if they don't deliver, how may city governments and the public legally respond?

Cable was a long time coming. Its function in the early fifties was to bring in a clear television picture and a greater selection of over-the-air television channels to areas of poor reception. In those days, it was known as Community Antenna Television, or CATV. The excitement over cable came with the discovery that the wire could provide channels in far greater number than the airwaves could, and that these channels might be used for a good deal more than light entertainment. For its social service potential, the new medium caught the fancy of social scientists, urban planners, community organizers, educators, and video enthusiasts. But most of them gave up on it when their ideas did not bear fruit overnight.

The seemingly extravagant visions for cable began to be dismissed in the early seventies as "blue sky," and the Spring 1972 issue of the *Yale Review of Law and Policy* was entirely devoted to what the magazine called "The Cable Fable." The industry itself became doubtful. And the first attempts to wire large cities—Manhattan, for example—were disconcerting. Urban cable construction was found to be far more expensive than rural construction. There were problems with landlords who wanted to be paid for letting cable in, as well as difficulties in gaining access to telephone poles and underground ducts. But the biggest problem of all was that urban residents did not need cable to improve reception. Most households could receive four or more channels with rabbit-ear or rooftop antennas, and therefore would not likely pay for the only service cable then had to sell. The development and delivery of cable's technological promise was stalled by a straightforward dilemma: The biggest and most lucrative markets had no need for a community antenna service. Planners and academicians offered suggestions on how to make cable desirable in the cities, but the real solution finally came from the commercial sector.

In 1975, Home Box Office (HBO), a small pay-television service, made a fateful decision to hitch its future to the RCA Satcom I satellite. Cable's resurgence traces to that single action, for what HBO achieved in transmitting its signal by satellite was an instant national network, one with distribution capabilities resembling those of ABC, CBS, and NBC, but at a fraction of the cost. Other companies quickly followed HBO's lead.

The RCA satellite soon became saturated with program services for cable systems—some for pay, some carrying advertising, and some designed to increase the attractiveness of the total cable package. For nonpay programming, cable systems spent a few cents per subscriber for the right to carry the network. With advertising-supported networks, the cable operator was allowed to sell some advertising locally.

But the simplest way to fill a channel by satellite was to use independent, large-city television stations specializing in cable's two biggest draws—sports and movies. Through cable and satellites, these local stations (WTBS Atlanta, WOR-TV New York, and WGN-TV Chicago, for example) all became nationally broadcast "superstations."

Because it carried HBO (the most popular service), RCA's Satcom I (now Satcom IIIR) became the main satellite for cable. In short order its twenty channels were claimed, and some have been subleased to programmers at handsome profits. Many prospective users are waiting for space, and others have booked transponders on Western Union's Westar satellite in hopes that cable systems would build a second earth station to take down its signals.

In addition to the shower of programming pouring from the satellite, cable has gained from technology such new applications as fire- and burglar-alarm systems; two-way communications capabilities that make shopping, banking, and polling possible by cable; and the use of the home television screen as a display terminal for printed information. Also, some cable systems are building special local networks to facilitate interchanges of visual materials and data between schools, hospitals, libraries, and municipal offices. The cable operator in 1980 therefore has what he lacked in the 1970s—important things to sell in the major cities. And this has incited the wild rush for big city franchises.

The systems that cable companies now propose to build in the large urban markets differ markedly from those constructed in the past. As early as 1963, twelve-channel cable came into regular use in rural areas. It remained standard until the early seventies, when new twenty-channel systems were built. Later, in Columbus, Ohio, a multifaceted system called Qube was developed by Warner Cable. This system has thirty channels, some of which let subscribers buy specific programs and participate in public-opinion polls. Qube has come to represent the state of the art, and no city considering franchise bids will settle for anything less.

By the end of 1979, 70 percent of all existing U.S. cable systems still had not changed their twelve-channel programming capacity. In new franchise offerings, however, channel capacity has rapidly climbed from forty to fifty-two, and in some cases, to more than one hundred. Virtually all bidders now offer the two-way and pay-per-program capabilities.

Subscribers can now buy new programming in several differently priced tiers of basic service. Typical tiers include combinations of over-the-air signals; satellite-delivered programming; informational, educational, and cultural material, and local-access channels. Cable has moved so far from its position of five years ago that today some companies give away their initial tier of basic service (which used to be cable's economic mainstay). Subscribers to this new-style cable may pay anywhere from nothing to $50 monthly for the services they select.

Such sophisticated cable systems are terribly expensive to construct. The wiring costs for cities like Cincinnati, St. Paul, and Omaha, with system sizes ranging from 110,000 to 160,000 homes, are expected to run up to $40 million. Dallas, with 400,000 homes, will cost $100 million.

Despite such costs, with the vast array of programming and services, few people doubt that high-capacity cable systems can be built and operated profitably in urban centers. But there remains a major question: Has the medium already been crippled by furious franchise competition, in which bidders must offer immense cash giveaways and low subscriber fees?

Since early 1979, bids on franchises have gone berserk: eighty or more channels of programming for just $10 a month; immediate prepayment to the municipality of the franchise fee in the amount of millions of dollars; purchasing of bonds issued by financially destitute municipalities; building and equipping of access centers; funding of foundations to support local programming; creation of tape libraries, and granting of substantial equity in the entire venture to people with political influence, to local civic groups, or to a city itself.

Obviously, this is not a game for the faint-hearted or cautious. Cities and cable companies blame each other for the current craziness. Monroe Rifkin, then president of American Television and Communications Corporation (ATC), told a gathering at the University of Wisconsin that the cable franchising process occurs in an environment "where excesses are encouraged and realism is penalized." At the same meeting, David Korte of the Cable Television Information Center, a nonprofit group that advises cities, put the shoe on the other foot. "The applicants are promising not only more than the city wants, but more than they are capable of delivering." It is not evident that cities are unhappy with the giveaway offers made by franchisees. But many do believe unrealistic promises are being made. If the promises cannot be kept, everyone stands to be harmed. As the highly respected journal, *Cable TV Regulation Newsletter,* said in August 1980, "Just when you think franchising competition has peaked and there is nothing left to offer, another summit is sighted and a new crest must be scaled. The future breathing space for a reasonable rate of return seems to be thinning."

Reviewing the six applications submitted for the Dallas franchise, the Cable Television Information Center criticized them all for not showing an adequate rate of return, which is most simply defined as the money a corporation has made on its capital investment after expenses and taxes have been paid. The financial consulting firm of Gary A. Dent Associates, analyzing the same Dallas bids and taking the bidders' own figures at face value, reported that, after twelve years of operations, rates of return on the projected investments for the entire period ran from 4.74 percent down to minus 5.32 percent, with three of the six bids showing rates of return of less than zero. Even if the system were sold after twelve years of operation, Dent figures indicated that the rate of return for all the bidders would be significantly less than the current cost of borrowing money. This approach is risky for any venture. But what makes the high-cost cable situation particularly alarming is the fact that the service is being so blithely merchandised, and its anticipated revenues so cheerfully toted up even before results are in. No cable system comparable to the type now being franchised has been built anywhere before. Both its costs and its potential dwarf those of existing systems. In addition, the demographics of the urban centers receiving the new cable are, generally, very different from the demographics of the medium-sized and small towns that until recently have been cable's principal market.

The limited amount of market experience gained in these smaller systems is not a reliable guide to the economics of big-city "supercable." No one really knows what services and offerings the subscriber to the new urban cable system will actually pay for.

Another complicating factor is that cable's rank among the electronic technologies to be unleashed on the American consumer in the eighties has not been fully established. Some of the technologies that may compete for at least part of the cable subscriber's time and dollar include video tape and video disc, direct broadcasting from satellite to home (DBS), and multipoint distribution service (MDS).

The last may be a real sleeper. MDS is a microwave common-carrier broadcasting technology that can disseminate television signals within a twenty-mile radius. Current FCC rules permit MDS stations to transmit two television channels in urban centers. MDS signals are principally beamed to hotels, motels, and business establishments, although operators have begun to solicit home hook-ups for the delivery of pay television. To receive MDS one must install a small microwave receiving dish and down-converter that cost around $250.

It takes $30 million to $200 million to bring cable to urban centers; MDS stations can be built and put on the air in the same areas for about $100,000. Moreover, there is no serious technical reason why the MDS transmission band could not be expanded for twenty or thirty television signals. Because it is a broadcasting technology MDS is regulated entirely at the federal level, so the local franchising situation has no effect on its installation. MDS operations can be established in any city, whether or not a cable system exists there.

Another competitor for some viewers is low-powered television broadcasting. This service, for which the FCC is now processing applications, will involve the licensing of hundreds of highly localized television stations throughout the country, each transmitting over relatively short distances. A 1978 FCC Task Force estimated that the cost of creating such a station, complete with minimal program origination facilities, would be $55,000. Low-powered stations are capable of providing many kinds of television service, including pay television.

To introduce high-cost cable into this volatile scene—especially with commitments that push projected rates of return to the vanishing point—is risky, to say the least. The cable franchising process needs to be greatly reformed, so that the public and private risks can be substantially reduced. It would be wise to curb the lavish giveaway promises made against unknown returns and to delay the introduction of new technology until it has undergone extensive market experimentation. Overall, there is a need for intelligent planning.

Unfortunately, each of those who could lead reform—city governments, access groups, and consumer advocates—stands to lose some of the cable operator's largesse if the system were to be improved. Most prefer the giveaways being offered to a more orderly and reasonable franchising procedure.

A front-page article in the March 10, 1980 issue of *access,* the publication of Ralph Nader's National Citizens Committee for Broadcasting (now Telecommunications Research and Action Center), summarized the current mood in making these recommendations for local action:

- Ask for twice the local channels the cable company offers;
- exact a high franchise fee;
- find out what is available in the finest cable systems today, and then ask for more.

Now that cable companies are realizing that local access groups will be making substantial demands, those companies are incorporating high-cost access projects, with large staffs, into their proposals.

By joining—and, in fact, leading—the every-man-for-himself

melee that now passes for national policy on cable, groups wearing the mantle of the public interest look more like part of the difficulty than part of the solution. The essential problem is the absence of any national policy on cable.

There are two well-established objectives of United States communications policy. The first is *establishment of a strong national pattern of communications.* The Communications Act of 1934, which created the FCC, states that the commission was formed, "for the purpose of regulating interstate and foreign commerce and communication by wire and radio so as to make available, so far as possible, to all people of the United States, a rapid, efficient, nationwide, and worldwide wire and radio communications service with adequate facilities at reasonable charges."

The second goal of communications policy, reflected in many of the FCC proceedings, is *the promotion of communications capabilities at the local level.* This objective was well stated by the President's 1968 Task Force on Communications Policy: "No aspect of communications policy is more important than measures or arrangements which would permit or encourage the growth of communications of all kinds within localities: the discussion of local issues; contact with local or regional political leaders; tapping local talent; the use of local resources in education, technology, sports, and the expression of all kinds of local interests."

Cable is capable of contributing much toward the realization of both these objectives, but the size and value of its contribution depends on how some urgent questions will be dealt with. Who will run these powerful communications systems, who will supervise, and for whose benefit? Who will have access rights to cable, for what purposes, and for the transmission of what kinds of material? Who will be turned away?

When I wrote *The Wired Nation* in 1970, I urged Congress to designate cable a common carrier, like the telephone system, satellite systems, and multipoint distribution service. Under this kind of regulation, owners of cable systems would forego all right to program them. Instead, they would lease channel time to all those who want to present programs, and the leasing would be done on a nondiscriminatory basis at standard posted rates. Cable would be available on the same first-come, first-served basis as the telephone. The cable system's owner would have no right to refuse any law-abiding customer. Everyone would have the right to be a cable broadcaster.

My proposal aroused a great deal of interest but produced no action. Now it may be too late to institute such a policy. In many large cities, cable franchises have already been granted with the understanding that the operator will choose the program networks and pay-television services the system will provide and that the operator will share in the proceeds from these services. Since the economic plan of these systems has been worked out on that basis, to change the rules drastically now would create chaos. Yet it is alarming that after all these years there still exists no mandate or structure to help determine a standard for access rights to cable.

All that had served as a structure were rules adopted by the FCC in 1972 requiring all new cable systems in urban centers to set aside one channel each for educational, governmental, and public use at no charge. Also required was a "leased access" channel on which the operator could sell time segments. But these rules were overturned by the federal courts in 1978 on the ground that no adequate basis for them existed in the Communications Act of 1934. The decision abrogated the federal government's right to require either commercial or noncommercial access to cable under existing law.

This leaves the matter up to Congress, but tides running in the national legislature appear to favor less, rather than more, government power to mandate access. A bill (S. 2827) introduced in the Senate in June 1980 would have given the cable operator control over all video services on his systems, thereby prohibiting municipalities from requiring access to cable systems in their franchises. The move was headed off, not because the Senate was unfriendly to the idea but because the National League of Cities filed a strong protest against any diminution of municipal franchising powers.

Ownership patterns pose another crucial set of questions. For example, the three major pay-television suppliers—Home Box Office, Showtime, and The Movie Channel—have ownership ties with large MSOs, the multiple-system operators of cable. Two of the three are also affiliated with program production companies—The Movie Channel with Warner Bros. TV and Showtime with Viacom Enterprises.

So each of these enterprises consists of a national supplier of pay programming and a large group of captive cable systems to which the programming can be distributed. Four of the top five—

six of the top ten—big cable companies in the United States are involved in these combines. And these same big cable companies have been capturing the lion's share of the new franchises being granted in major cities. Of the ten big-city franchises granted since the beginning of 1979, seven were conferred on companies involved in these combines, and in an eighth city, sections containing approximately half the population went to one of these companies through purchase and acquisition, after the franchises were granted.

As cable comes to the cities, power is being consolidated by companies that are already large and already heavily involved in ownership and programming. Since the courts have ruled that the FCC has no power to require access to cable, these companies are free to do as they wish about granting access on their cable systems to new competitors in the programming field. Even where access is granted, the combine controls the marketing of all programming and services. It would not likely promote the programming of a strong competitor if that meant helping the rival make a dent in the national marketplace.

Interestingly, the arrangements now being left to take root in the cable industry bear strong resemblance to the arrangement the government outlawed for movie companies. In the film industry's earlier days, several of the major film studios also owned large theater chains. They used this marriage of exhibition and distribution to control ticket prices and to exclude competing films from their theaters. In 1948 a Justice Department consent decree put an end to such ownership arrangements, forcing the movie studios to divest themselves of theater chains. Now, through the new electronic media, the centralized control of programming, distribution, and exhibition is sneaking back into the marketplace.

Yet another issue in the coming of the wired nation, and perhaps the most enigmatic of all, is the role to be played by the telephone company. Ma Bell is at present not involved in cable. The FCC ruled in 1970 that telephone companies cannot build and operate cable systems in areas they provide with telephone service, except in rural situations where telephone company construction is the only feasible alternative.

However, with their tremendous switching capability (which can be applied to two-way cable communications), and with their increasing experience in laying and operating fiber-optic cable, telephone companies are obviously capable of building high-capacity cable systems anywhere. Indeed, some people may consider it desirable to have one wire coming into the home—carrying both telephone and cable—rather than two discrete wires.

The real question is not technological but philosophical. Should Ma Bell be allowed to bring its massive economic power and leverage into this field? If so, under what kind of regulation and with what restrictions?

These questions are not likely to be raised by the American Telephone & Telegraph Company, which has repeatedly said it has no interest in entering the field of cable television. The parties most likely to pose them are the elected officials of some large city at some not-too-distant moment. Weary of franchising battles and giveaways, uncertain whether the offers they receive now will prove financially unrealistic later—or disillusioned to find, after granting a franchise, that the company can't or won't deliver what it promised—the officials in such a city may petition the FCC for something new: that AT&T be licensed to build and operate a common-carrier cable system in their city, something it could accomplish quickly. If and when that happens, how should the goverment respond?

Just when such issues are being pushed more urgently to the forefront of the public agenda by cable's growth, Washington is caught up in the new doctrine of deregulation. The prevailing idea in the capital today is that commerce is better regulated by the marketplace than by government bureaucrats. This has prompted the FCC to disband its Cable Television Bureau and abandon most of its regulatory structure for cable.

As with all philosophies of public policy, deregulation has merit and important uses but tends to be overapplied. It is too easily used in place of thought and planning. And it is notably inapplicable to cable because, as a practical matter, deregulation cannot be achieved by removing only the federal presence. This is because two additional levels of regulation—state and local—lie between cable television and the marketplace. Cancellation of the federal role merely shifts responsibility to the states and municipalities, where there is neither the mandate nor the equipment to formulate rules with a view to the national interest.

Right now, it is essential that the federal government move back into cable regulation and remain there. The FCC should not, and undoubtedly would not, repeat its old mistake of imposing highly detailed and complicated regulations on cable. What is really needed now is a national charter for this important new medium—one that would provide broad outlines for the industry's structure. This is not a task to be left to the FCC, which has struggled in the past to reconcile new technologies and old laws and repeatedly was challenged in the courts.

If cable is to grow sensibly and in ways that contribute to national communications goals, the responsibility falls to the Congress and the president of the United States.

2.

The Twists in Two-Way Cable

David Burnham

Within a hundred minutes after the televised debate between President Reagan and former President Carter in the fall of 1980, three-quarters of a million Americans flashed their thumbs up-thumbs down verdict to an electronic voting booth set up by the American Telephone & Telegraph Company for the news division of the American Broadcasting Company. It was the world's largest and fastest public-opinion survey.

Though the ABC survey was conceptually and technically flawed, similar polls will almost certainly become a force in America's political and commercial life. Already, politicians, news organizations, and entertainment shows in Columbus, Ohio, and other cities are harvesting public feelings about issues ranging from energy to homosexuality—with the help of Qube, an experimental electronic system soon to be ubiquitous in the United States.

The ability to collect and tabulate the almost immediate reactions of millions of Americans to a specific event or problem could ultimately reduce today's prevalent cynical alienation. But it could just as easily lead to a serious weakening of many existing institutions in representative government—and to a gradual erosion in the independent judgment and leadership of public officials.

Two-way interactive television presents these starkly contrast-

21

ing opportunities for good and evil. It is a computer-powered system that lets the subscriber answer, through his television, any multiple choice questions he is asked, or order any goods and services he is offered. The home terminal of this electronic umbilical cord is a small plastic keyboard, about the size of a thick paperback novel, attached to the family set. When responding to a question, the subscriber "touches in" on one of a series of buttons, the central computer swiftly calculates the proportion of the audience preferring the various options, and the answer is displayed on the home screen.

The interactive television subscriber can also wire his home with sophisticated security and health-monitoring devices, and can increase the number of entertainment, news, and educational programs already piped into his living room.

Dreamy blue-sky speculation about interactive television and its potential has increased markedly over the past decade. But 500,000 homes will probably be wired by 1984—many millions more by the late eighties—so the wave of the future is about to crash on the beach of reality.

Optimistic futurists and executives selling two-way television have eloquently enumerated the ways the system can enrich America's cultural life, improve the responsiveness of government bureaucracies, and even solve the national energy crisis by eliminating the need to drive to the shopping center or town meeting. The perils, however, have largely been ignored. Some problems:

Instant Polling—Two-way television's technical ability to take the pulse of the body politic creates an almost irresistible desire to undertake such polls. But if ABC News was willing to ask the nation who won the 1980 presidential beauty contest, why won't ABC News or some other organization decide to measure the nation's mood the next time some country decides to seize a group of American diplomats? And how would such unreflective and necessarily ill-informed opinion influence the actions of the politician then occupying the White House, or the response of the nation holding the hostages?

Personal Privacy—With a fully developed two-way system, many significant details about the life of the subscribing family will be funneled through the system's computer. The information collected by such a computer might well include messages sent by electronic mail to a stockbroker or travel agent, various banking transactions, books ordered at the local bookstore or library, hours devoted to pay-per-view programs that might include soft-core pornography, and the comings and goings of security-service subscribers. Though such details are now frequently recorded by separate organizations, the concentration of data in the computer of one privately owned company presents a major snooping hazard.

Collective Privacy—Even if laws and procedures provide each subscriber an ironclad guarantee that personal information will never be improperly shared, neighborhood patterns of book reading, television watching, banking, and electronic shopping will give commercial and political marketing experts a powerful new tool to use on the psyches of unsuspecting customers. When the information collected by the two-way system's computer is merged with the Census Bureau's tract-by-tract information, super salesmen will be able to target their ever-more-refined pitches only at the most susceptible consumers.

Information Deprivation—The services offered by two-way interactive television are expensive. As such systems become more and more essential in the delivery of cultural, educational, and political information, will the service's price further widen the gap that already separates the poor from the rest of society? Behind this issue lies a complex debate about whether two-way television systems should continue to be owned and operated by traditional business organizations or whether they should be regulated.

Blurring—With the enormous increase in the number of channels entering subscribers' homes comes a diversified selection of programs. One experimental show in Columbus is called the "infomercial," a combination of objective documentary and paid commercial. Some consumer experts fear the marriage of the two forms might do nothing more than mislead and confuse. Lurking behind their concern is the broad question of editorial responsibility. Should the owners of two-way cable systems be considered similar to newspaper publishers and granted First Amendment rights and obligations? Or should cable systems be likened to the telephone company and be required to carry any message an individual wants to send?

Regulation—New government agencies are the traditional panacea for serious social problems in America. But where fragile matters like freedom of speech and privacy are at stake, the cure might well end up being more serious than the disease. Curiously, that possibility has not stopped Sweden, France, and several other European countries from establishing strong government agencies to inspect and license the very computerized information bases that need protection. The prospect of a similar fox being asked to guard the chicken-house in the United States may well be the communication boom's ultimate ironic threat. The dimming but nevertheless powerful memories of the Watergate years remind us that government agencies sometimes abuse their powers.

All this talk of unchecked communications growth and the problems it could cause irritates Gustave M. Hauser, a principal godfather of two-way television's commerical development. "Tony Oettinger, the Harvard professor, got it right at a seminar in Cambridge last year," he said. "Perils, perils, perils. If we keep worrying about all the perils, we're going to be paralyzed."

Hauser, a Harvard-trained lawyer and former senior executive in the independent telephone industry, has just departed as chief executive of Warner Amex Cable Communications, Inc. It is Warner Amex, a subsidiary of the entertainment conglomerate Warner Communications and the American Express Company, that has pioneered commercial development of two-way television in Columbus and is now installing similar systems in Houston, Cincinnati, Pittsburgh, and Dallas.

The far-reaching potential of two-way television (which other companies have been forced to offer cities in hopes of gaining territorial franchises) has deeply fired Scott Kurnit, the tall, bearded, and faintly Mephistophelean vice president for Qube programming at Warner Amex. "I think interactive television can be an enormously beneficial social instrument," Kurnit said during an interview. "The unrelieved passiveness of traditional television broadcasting has had a significant negative impact on the American family and the American community. Interactive television will allow people to have fuller, freer lives, to communicate with each other, to learn how to work with each other. The system lessens isolation because it almost requires members of the family or community to consult with each other before deciding on important issues."

The Qube system offers two other television services in addition to the interactive one. First, Qube's subcribers in Columbus have at their disposal an enormous number of programs—approximately 720 hours in every 24-hour day. Second, because of the system's design, specialized programs can be offered to appropriate subscribers. A highly technical medical course, for example, cannot be seen by regular subscribers, but only by physicians signed up for the training. The system can also insure that televised town meetings only be aired in affected townships, where subscribers can use their Qube keypads to answer their mayor's questions directly.

"The idea, our goal, is to offer sufficient programming so that every member of our community can satisfy his separate needs every moment of the day," Kurnit said as he flipped through the thirty channels currently available to Columbus subscribers. (Newer systems offer even more channels.) Together we briefly inspected some of the varied offerings: the channel providing a twenty-four-hour-a-day news program; another showing round-the-clock movies; a third featuring old television shows with their commercials removed; a fourth carrying children's programs; and another channel offering soft-core pornography. The special pay-per-view features—like a major boxing match or the Ohio State University football games not carried on regular television—were of course not available that weekday afternoon.

Neither were any of the Columbus system's experimental programs. One of them is a monthly show giving viewers a chance to take part in a discussion about books. It is unlike any discussion show on conventional television, as the audience is frequently asked multiple-choice questions about the book under discussion, and is given an opportunity to vote on which one of five books should be the subject of next month's program. Any participant, furthermore, can telephone in while the discussion is underway, ask an appropriate question, or call for a change of subject matter—and the proposal will immediately be put to the rest of the audience. One final wrinkle: After the book for next month's discussion has been selected, viewers interested in preparing for the talk can receive a loaned copy from the Columbus Public Library simply by pressing a button. Their response tells the central computer to include their names and addresses on a distribution list for the library's use.

"The book club is in many ways the most interesting and exciting use of interactive television now on Qube," said Tom Harnish, who, with his wife, Judy, has worked at a Columbus-based non-profit organization that operates an on-line computer network used by more than 2,300 libraries. Neither is noticeably uncomfortable with America's high-tech society. But sitting in the second-floor den watching Scott Kurnit as he led an early-evening interactive discussion about government regulation, both indicated they had some reservations about Qube.

"One aspect that worries me," said Harnish, puffing on his pipe, "is what happens to those who are not able to pay the $15 or $20 a month for Qube, the possibility that we may be creating a new kind of underclass. I remember I once worked in a hospital in Baltimore where medical treatment was pretty easy to get as long as you had a telephone. But you would be surprised at how many people living in a big city are so poor or disconnected that they don't have a telephone."

And Harnish added that there is precious little interactive television now being offered by the Columbus cable system. "They bill Qube as two-way interactive, but there aren't very many hours of interactive each week and some of the programs so labeled tend to ask trivial questions, such as whether you wear eyeglasses."

Gustave Hauser, the Warner Amex executive, at first brushed aside a question on the extent of Qube's commitment to interactive television. "No, no, no," he replied when asked how many hours of such television were scheduled each day. "You can't judge it that way. Television is not based on tonnage, it's based on quality. The number of hours is irrelevant. You can put a dog in front of a camera and you have a show, but you don't have a program."

After further pressing, however, Hauser said Qube was now programming "several hours of interactive television each day. But some days we might do none. It depends upon what we want to spend our money on. Everything is a question of economics. I can't schedule eighteen hours of interactive every day. It requires too many people. Everything is relative to economics, and the economics is changing because there will be advertising and other sources of revenue, particularly if we do market research programs."

The question of economics—what the subscribers and advertisers are willing to pay for—of course bears on every issue concerning two-way television. And because the service is totally new, developing at a tremendous speed, and affecting American life in ways as yet only dimly perceived, it is hard for the public to know what problems the system may pose—and therefore what safeguards are worth buying. In a speech before the Union League Club of New York City, Charles D. Ferris, chairman of the Federal Communications Commission during the Carter years, tried to awaken the public to threats against personal privacy. "The fundamental problem I see with the coming information age," he warned, is that it "will rob us of one of our more important rights in a free society, the right to privacy."

When American families are wired for two-way television and its ancillary services, he went on, "a computer will have a record of what they buy and how much they spend. It will know whether they pay their bills quickly, slowly, or not at all, and it will know where their money comes from. It will know whether they watched the debates, or the football game, or a controversial movie. It will know when they came home the previous night— and probably in what condition, depending on how many alarms they accidentally set off. It will know how many people are in their houses and in what rooms. In other words, it will know more about them than anyone should."

What's to be done? Many knowledgeable experts believe that mechanical or legal safeguards can be developed. "In my own view, privacy is something of a wash," said Harry M. Shooshan, III, the former chief counsel of the House Communications Subcommittee. "Of course, there are problems, but there are also ways technology can enhance personal security."

Charles L. Jackson, Shooshan's partner in a Washington consulting firm, worked on the same House subcommittee as chief engineer. "The technology gives us an opportunity to enhance privacy as well as undercut it," Jackson said during a conversation in the small firm's new office. "As the system is being built, you can choose the ends that will be served. I do not believe that reliance on the technology by itself creates the hazard to privacy. The question is, what are the goals and what are the values of the people who are creating that system?"

Jackson had to acknowledge, however, that privacy is a subtle issue. "Somehow, we want an assurance that someone who is a political dissident—whether it's John Anderson or even Abbie Hoffman—can live his life without fear his political opponents will someday be handed a detailed report on his private behavior."

Warner Amex's Hauser emphasized the concern he felt about the privacy of Qube customers. "I am concerned, others are concerned, we should all be concerned," he said. But like many lawyers, he saw the savior in the law, rather than in technology. "If there is an abuse, there will be a regulation. I am delighted to have any regulation that is appropriate. Why don't we see what the public wants before we start regulating the business? Why don't we build the system and then worry about the things we don't like in it? The people who want to regulate in advance are the people who are going to prevent progress."*

The seriousness of the privacy threat, and suggested remedies for it, generate much disagreement. But two-way television's instant polling capability evokes a much more unified sense of concern. "There, there lies the potential for a real problem," said Shooshan. "The media too much dominate the political environment today. If a mayor can take a poll over two-way television about any issue he wants, he can significantly erode the powers of an elected city council or the intent of state referendum laws, which require a certain number of signatures before an issue can be put on a ballot for a direct decision by the voters."

"Instant polling is an area of enormous peril," said Sidney W. Dean, a longstanding member of New York's advisory committee on cable television. "Instantaneous surveys on public-policy issues are frightening for a number of reasons. First, there is no time for thoughtful consideration of the issue. Second, from my long experience in marketing research, I know that the hand that writes the questions usually begets the answers."

Robert W. Ross is a young, aggressive, and highly articulate senior vice president of the National Cable Television Association. "The consequences? All the consequences are positive," was Ross's reply to a question about the ultimate impact of the cable industry on Americans. "Information is like nuclear power. You can harness it for good or you can harness it for evil. It depends upon what kind of regulatory structures are set up and how the regulations are applied." But he was far less reassuring when our conversation turned to what he ironically called "the era of plebiscitary democracy." This era will have arrived, he said, the day a politician can say "push button three if you agree with me, and seventeen million hit button three and the decision is made to lock up the Nisei."

Ross recounted his experiences as an ensign in Vietnam, where he believes the nearly instantaneous communication links with Washington robbed him and the rest of the officers of the appropriate authority to make decisions. "If the time comes when an elected official has the abililty to swiftly determine how his

---

*Note: In 1981, Warner Amex adopted a "Code of Privacy," a set of ethical guidelines it pledges to follow in operating its two-way systems.

constituents feel about any issue he is dealing with, it is my guess that the individuality and self-confidence of that official will be undermined," he warned. "A congressman is there to represent his constituents, not just to do his own will. On the other hand, it is simultaneously important for politicians to exercise their own judgments about the rightness of something, rather than responding to pressures of the mob or emotions of the moment."

As two-way interactive cable is installed in a significant number of American homes, many of its fundamental perils—Constitutional, economic, and philosophical—become evident. And Ithiel de Sola Pool, a professor at the Massachusetts Institute of Technology, worries that society might overreact to these perils. "No democracy would tolerate the notion that a reporter's notebook be licensed and subject to inspection by those he is writing about," Pool said. "No democracy would tolerate that a political party's campaign plans be treated the same way, nor that our correspondence with our friends abroad should be compulsorily opened up. But that is exactly what many countries are requiring for computer files. What then happens when a reporter keeps his files on his home computer, or when a political party produces its plans on an intelligent word-processor, or when we write our friends by electronic mail?"

Pool noted the laws passed by several European countries. He warned darkly that "a Luddite fear of the computer" is intensifying the centuries of struggle for the protection of personal freedom.

At a time when technological changes are placing large and unanticipated pressures on society, choosing the right course is hard business. Consultant Harry Shooshan recalled Lord Devlin's telling comment about the dangers of our difficult and subtle times: "If freedom of the press or freedom of speech perishes, it will not be by sudden death. It will be a long time dying from a debilitating disease caused by a series of erosive measures, each of which, if examined singly, would have a great deal to be said for it."

3.

The Man Who Started the New Television

Jonathan Black

Once upon a time, not very long ago, Home Box Office was a mere memorandum scuttling across executive desks on the thirty-fifth floor of Time Inc. headquarters. It was not a memo taken with utter seriousness. Who, after all, would *pay* to see movies or sports at home? Television's very allure had been to bring news and entertainment, free, into the American living room. So the Cassandras gloated and whispered among themselves about the most perplexing stranger brought in to midwife the notion. The man was not, for starters, a Time Inc-er. Nor had he served even one day's time in the business. This man was a Wall Street attorney. A former Bible student. A thirty-three-year-old engineering buff whose firm built irrigation ditches and dams in developing countries. But give credit to the powers that hired him. No one has had a more vital, radical influence on pay television, cable—and ultimately, perhaps the networks—than Gerald Levin.

Decades hence, when the history of television is told, Levin will still be renowned for his seminal matchmaking feat: that explosive and highly fertile marriage of cable and satellite. Spawned under the astrological sign of Satcom I (now Satcom IIIR), HBO's heavenly signal begat pay, and pay, with remarkable speed, begat the wired nation. Suddenly the dozing cable industry awoke from its early-seventies doldrums with a hot new product to penetrate urban markets. Once, the smug triumvirate of network television ignored the wired competition. Those networks are smug no more.

Consider one fact: In 1980, Time Inc.'s Video Group—led by HBO and Time's cable company, American Television & Communications—earned more than the entire NBC network. And consider the remarkable changes Levin wrought: Henry Luce's vast publishing and forestry empire has become, in terms of both earnings and capital spending, a cable company—with trees demoted to second place and magazines to third.

Levin might seem a most improbable star to have engineered such an upheaval. Unimposing is perhaps the most apt word to characterize a man who, in both style and personality, more closely resembles an assistant bank manager than a flashy television executive. He's the kind of man, says one acquaintance, who always introduces himself for fear he won't be remembered. At CBS or NBC, his quiet, dogged efforts would have earned him a high roost in accountancy. Only at Time Inc., where glitter and glamour come second to solid, buttoned-down smarts, could Levin have emerged as he has—a visionary giant. In many ways, Levin is the Lenin of video, its bookish seer, a man who prefers to stress "the force of ideas" rather than his own impact, a man who toiled with talmudic attention to detail, and to his and everyone else's surprise, forged a revolution. "He's one hell of a commodity," says J. Richard Munro, Time Inc.'s president and chief executive officer. "We have not seen that many Jerry Levins in this building."

Levin first entered the building in April 1972, hired to explore the concept of pay television for Sterling Cable Network, the partially owned Time Inc. subsidiary, in the hope that pay would improve growth and help amortize costs. Just seven months later, on a wretched rainy November night, that idea became reality when 365 homes in Wilkes Barre, Pennsylvania, were able to tune in a New York Rangers hockey game and the film *Sometimes a Great Notion*. And where was Levin on that night full of portent (so stormy that HBO's microwave transmitter collapsed and was repaired just twenty-five minutes before the inaugural feed)? Quite typically, he was busy wrestling in the realm of ideas, holed up alone in HBO's humble annex, playing furniture mover in an effort to grasp the night's implications. Out went the sterile office desks, and in came a comfy couch and coffee table—an ersatz den lit by borrowed table lamps.

"I was trying to simulate a living room, I wanted to know how it *felt.*" And living-room viewing felt, well, remarkable. "It wasn't just the lack of commercials or the first curse word. It was a new dynamic of the medium. That night I knew we had something significant. Something powerful."

Levin's glimpse that night of something powerful did not shake the world, or even the cable industry. Indeed, HBO was so undefined, and pay television was viewed with such wariness, that when the company urgently needed a program director, Levin aborted the talent hunt and assumed the job himself, adding it to his already cumbersome title—director of finance, administration, and transmission. Navigating those early days of HBO required a rather awesome repertoire of skills; it was a time when vision often counted less than a talent for prowling through facts and figures. There were tariffs to calculate, microwave routes to plot, gloomy projections to refute. And into this swamp of detail Levin waded with poise and patience. "There were days when lesser people would have jumped out a window," Munro remembers. "But Jerry wasn't a screamer or table-banger. He hid his emotions very well. I still find his coolness remarkable."

Praise befitting a true Time Inc-er. Up in the nether reaches of corporate headquarters, where a modest manner and solid managerial grasp denote character, Levin is much admired for his lack of fanaticism. "Jerry lives and breathes video twenty-four hours a day," says Robbin Ahrold, an early Levin cohort at HBO. "But he's not the kind of guy who's here at six every morning and leaves at ten at night. He's not a compulsive. He's not *obsessed.*"

An obsessed personality would not have survived the endless series of critical decisions that marked those nascent years of HBO. Though some mistakes were tolerable, cushioned by Time Inc.'s uncommon marketing power, Levin steered a remarkably error-free course. As programming architect he was quick to see that if pay television had a future, it had to crack a powerful habit structure, prolong a viewer's attention span, and offer unique fare not available on commercial television. He recognized early the limited grab of regional sports, and keyed HBO to movies. (Later, with bucks and clout, he would engineer another major shift, from feature films, over which Time Inc. had little control, to homegrown non-movie material—entertainment specials.) As marketeer, Levin took the appropriate "high road" approach, positioning HBO in an insular, quality slot.

And how would HBO charge its subscribers? All other pay-programming experiments had toyed with pay-per-view. Ever a keen observer of the American living room, Levin realized that few viewers could cope with a buying decision every two hours, and conceived the monthly subscription service. And it was Levin, faced with another crucial fork in the road, who chose the correct path in developing HBO's relation to affiliates.

Of two basic options, the more obvious one was to lease channels from cable operators, and maintain control of installation, service, and marketing. For a corporate giant like Time, it was tempting to consolidate power high on the thirty-fifth floor. In the early 1970s, however, the wired nation still resembled a medieval fiefdom, with each cable-operator prince in his own domain. These were prideful pioneers, and Levin knew not to disturb their sovereignty. Better to go the second route: Leave the key marketing decisions to the local man who knew his audience and territory best. Build a partnership, not a hostile landlord-tenant relation. The choice wasn't as evident as it seemed. An early HBO competitor, Optical Sytems, went the other way and was soon gone from the business.

In forging the HBO affiliates network, Levin was a thoughtful strategist. And he was no less adroit at the critical task of selling HBO within the company. "He was incredibly persuasive when it came to obtaining funding here," says N.J. Nicholas, Levin's handpicked programming chief, who later succeeded to the HBO chairmanship. "He was evangelical, but he always put *numbers* beside his exhortations. That was key. How many businesses don't exist because the guy with the great ideas couldn't sell it?" From the start, Levin's exhortations left a vivid impression on Time management. Munro can still recall his first presentation: "Here was this guy talking about something and no one even knew what he was talking about. But we were all overwhelmed, awed. When the meeting was over, Andrew (Heiskell, former Time chairman) pulled me aside and said, 'Who *was* that guy?'"

Encountering Levin today, it's not hard to see why Heiskell left the meeting scratching his head. Levin's single idiosyncrasy—a moustache, too bushy to fit any corporate dicta—belies his lack of flourish. Indeed it's this lack of flash that makes him so curious, and so credible. There's no cheap showmanship about the man, no florid pretension or hoopla. Perched a bit stiffly on his office couch, he begins, even before a question is asked, weaving a devilishly seductive argument for the Video Group's current pet project: made-for-pay-television movies. Levin sees these as filling a gap, or as he puts it, "an aperture." Network television films are fine but limited—generally consigned to a $2 million budget, limited by built-in commercial breaks, and geared to television stars. Theatrical films, with their huge budgets and vast promotion, must rely increasingly on a kiddie audience. Between the two, Levin infers a "lost theatergoing public," adults hungry for serious fare. According to Arbitron, families—not just cable subscribers—go to fewer movies. They stay at home. Enter HBO, the premiere pay service that some think tops in quality and diversity, and that now must maintain its Number One rank with *programming*—which is, incidentally, a *major* source of revenue for the Hollywood film studios. Uttering such phrases as, "The critical mass is now there in terms of revenue-bearing potential," Levin moves from demography to distribution to philosophy with the ease of a man whose brain neurons seemed to carry extra charge and capacity. It's a case that he states so confidently, and with such level-headed fervor, that one quickly forgets that the yellow-brick road from broadcasting to movies is strewn with such warm corporate bodies as CBS and Westinghouse. Didn't *The Great Santini*—solid fare—flop at the box office only to be reborn on HBO? Levin suddenly makes it seem quite possible that HBO could rescue television from the crunch of network tripe and bloated studio spectaculars.

"I never came away from a conversation with Jerry in which I didn't learn something," says Peter Gross, an early Levin recruit to Time Inc. "He has tremendous intellectual aggression, tremendous curiosity. He's a true Renaissance figure. I assume you know about his encyclopedic reading . . ."

How did a Renaissance literate manage to crack the highly competitive, stratified corporate temple of Time Inc.? With very little fanfare. Though Levin's biography is remarkable for its frequent lurches in career, he is one of those enviable men who seem to have intuited a secret path whose every twist and turn leads, inevitably, to that satisfying station they'd quietly plotted all along. Born in Philadelphia in 1939, Levin grew up an avid sports and movie buff, toyed with an engineering career, "but always knew I wanted to be in business" (with those predispositions, HBO might have had him indentured right then). Majoring in philosophy and biblical literature, he graduated Phi Beta Kappa from Haverford College, attended the University of Pennsylvania

Law School (he was note editor of the Law Review), then joined New York's Simpson Thacher & Bartlett—the prestigious law firm that, coincident with the show-biz glimmer in Levin's eye, represented Paramount Pictures and several cable companies. Roy Reardon, a senior partner, recalls Levin with the familiar litany of praise and respect: "He was extremely smart, a superb lawyer. He was more of a generalist than most and could have moved in any direction. Confident but never pushy, a real gentleman. There was very little bullshit about him."

After four years with ST&B, deciding he wanted to "switch from law to management," Levin signed on as staff counsel with the Development & Resources Corporation, a consulting firm that works extensively in developing countries on projects ranging from engineering to public health—not the detour it seemed. Even a year spent in Iran, where DRC built a dam for the Shah, served Levin well during the early years at HBO: "It helped that I wasn't intimidated by technology. After all, the movement of electrons isn't that different from the movement of electricity."

In 1971, having risen to become general manager and chief operating officer at DRC, Levin gathered his credentials and took direct aim at Time Inc. "It was a conscious decision. Movies, sports, and TV had always been my avocation, so I decided to get into the business on the cable side. I was friendly with some people at Madison Square Garden who put me in touch with [Sterling Cable's] Chuck Dolan. Our first meeting convinced me that I had to give it a shot."

During the next few years, Levin's friends often fretted about his chosen target—and with good reason. There were times when HBO seemed doomed, and pay television an idea whose time had not yet come. In 1973, HBO had planned a promotional gimmick for the National Cable Television Association (NCTA) convention—a clock that would tick off the hourly gain in subscribers—but the idea was scrapped when Levin realized subscribership had begun to decline. Later that same year, Levin took a rare vacation, knowing he'd have to return to the building with a close-out plan. Happily subscribership crept up, but by the spring of 1975, HBO could count just a hundred thousand homes in only four states and had the unmistakable smell of yet another Time Inc. video fiasco. In 1972, assessing the future of television as glum, the powers at Time Inc. sold their stations in Denver, Indianapolis, San Diego, and Minneapolis to McGraw-Hill, only to see the industry revive, and watch, red-faced, while McGraw-

Hill made a bundle. Displaying a similar knack for bad timing, Time invested heavily in cable—just before cable hit its dog days in the early seventies. By the mid-seventies, HBO threatened to bomb as badly as another Time video goof, Hotelvision, and doubt on the thirty-fifth floor seemed terminal. "I despaired of the thing ever taking hold," remembers HBO's Ahrold. "I just didn't think it would go."

Where it went was up on "the Bird" —and the idea totally reversed the fortunes of both HBO and the cable industry. Or, as Levin modestly demurs: "We've never had a totally original idea here. It was the *linkage,* putting two disparate ideas together." That linkage was the marriage of HBO to RCA's Satcom I satellite.

In retrospect, the satellite decision looks inevitable. HBO circa 1975 faced a technological barrier to growth in its reliance on a cumbersome relay of microwave hops. To continue building a terrestrial network would have proved highly expensive and, with its stress on regional hubs, would have thwarted the *national* promise that meant so much at Time Inc. Explains Munro: "The risk-reward ratio sort of screamed for a satellite."

Maybe so. But the risks were still considerable. Merely by renting one Satcom I transponder, Time Inc. was gambling $7.5 million on precious few subscribers—and the rent would have to be paid whether ten viewers, or ten million, signed up. Satellite technology itself was still relatively untested: Prior to HBO's venture, use of the Bird was limited to single transmissions (from London to New York, for instance), whereupon the signals had to be distributed via land lines. Would blanket transmissions work? Would enough cable operators invest in enough earth stations? (Only two existed in 1975.) What about tariffs? It was no man's land. And perhaps the most dangerous pitfall lurked at the Federal Communications Commission. To this day, Levin wonders why the networks never bothered to file an FCC objection to HBO's application, a delaying tactic that might soon have proved fatal given HBO's rocky finances. So give Levin credit for selling the thirty-fifth floor, so effectively that Munro now calls it a "prudent business decision."

And give Levin credit for pitching the scheme to the UA-Columbia cable system in Vero Beach, Florida. "Why did he come to us? I don't know," says Robert Rosencrans, UA-Columbia president. "I assume he thought we'd be most likely to understand the idea. He probably thought he could get a quick decision."

Quick was an understatement. Levin called Rosencrans Friday.

On Monday morning Rosencrans called him back. Two weeks later, Levin was able to walk into the 1975 NCTA convention and announce that HBO had a cable operator to take the service and would be up on the satellite September 30. Remembering that epic announcement, a rare shiver of emotion thrills Levin's voice: "It was the compelling nature of the *idea,* its ripple effect. The impact was palpable, you could feel it, *taste* it . . ."

That ripple effect began to make the going easier. On September 30, the 12,500-mile feed of the Ali-Frazier fight in the Phillippines was truly a "thrilla from Manila" for a cable industry that had lost its spark. At Time Inc., the Bird turned HBO from a publishing empire's poor stepchild into a favorite son. With the simultaneous signal beamed from Satcom I, HBO could finally claim itself a true video network—a vision even Henry Luce's print minions respected. And by 1977, a pivotal year for both Levin and HBO, the thirty-fifth floor could at last rejoice with a measure of confidence: The FCC had just approved use of the small four-and-a-half-meter dish, opening the way for cable operators to join the service cheaply and effectively; in May of that year, the 100th earth station joined the network; in March, the U.S. Court of Appeals overturned a key FCC decision restricting pay-television programming content; in April, HBO's Bette Midler special won the first NCTA pay-television program award; and in October, with close to a million subscribers, HBO turned its first profit.

Today, that milestone seems like ancient history. HBO subscribers now number nearly eleven million, and Time Inc. can boast control of more than 60 percent of the pay-television market. Just as important, HBO throws off a tremendous cash-flow profit—rare, and highly useful in the capital-intensive cable industry. Spurred by HBO's success, Time has methodically bought control of the multiple-system owner ATC, which now counts more than two million subscribers, making Time the nation's largest cable operator. On top of these two wildly profitable video ventures sits Levin, who was promoted in 1979 to vice president of the Video Group—the umbrella division that also includes Time's million-subscriber movie channel, Cinemax. In 1980, the Video Group was granted almost one-third of Time's entire capital spending, a fact that hints at the internal clout Levin now wields. For instance, an experiment with a twenty-four-hour teletext service in San Diego that will allow customers to retrieve print information on their television screens is being run by Levin's Video Group, and not by Time's print honchos. "We have taken our place internally," says Levin. "It's still hard for people in the building to get used to the culture shock."

By the look of things, Levin will continue to send gentle shock waves through Time Inc. headquarters. Strengthening the role played by cable, he managed to fold Time-Life Films (which suffered 1980 pre-tax losses of $18 million, charged to the Video Group's earnings). "In theatrical films," explains Levin, "you have to be a major player. And if you're in motion pictures, you better be a distributor. To start a theatrical distribution business—well, we're looking into the future here, not the past." The Time-Life Cassette Club is also finished ("because basically cassettes are going rental . . . and because the mail-order business isn't big enough"). Announcing their demise, Levin seems decidedly pleased. More energy and bucks available for ATC and HBO—the launch pad for new programming.

After made-for-pay-television movies, Levin's next horizon is theater—new drama commissioned, staged, and distributed exclusively by HBO. Though nothing is definite, Levin hints at such big-name playwrights as Arthur Miller. He would like to focus increasingly on documentaries and, as always, discerns a vital perceptual gap between commercial and pay television: "Network documentaries work in a very narrow mold. They have a particular *feel*. But there's a fascinating chemistry that occurs when you take a pre-existent program format and mate it with pay. It's just one more marvel of this medium."

Though Levin doesn't anticipate the demise of network television, he does see it being forced to adapt and concentrate on "what it does best": news, sports, sitcoms. Only mildly flattered when HBO, after a decade of struggle and angst, is termed the "fourth network," Levin promptly cites research indicating that viewers go first to their HBO folio, and *then* consult the network channels. "But even HBO isn't enough," he adds. "Already viewers want more than one pay service."

Is Levin worried that the dazzling success of HBO and the ravenous video appetite it has spawned may have created a nation of stay-at-home television zombies? Yes, he acknowledges, a little. But he prefers to think he has "domesticated the TV set," given viewers the chance for intelligent choices, made people "TV-smart." "We are redefining the way the American people relate to their television set," says Levin with that quiet urgency that bears so much attention.

4.

Stanley Hubbard and His Magnificent New Video Flying Machine

Julie Talen

In the pea-green basement cafeteria of KSTP-TV, where its president and owner, Stan Hubbard, eats nearly every lunch, conversation turns to the recent pregnancy of a Twin Cities star anchorwoman, KSTP's own Cyndy Brucato. Hubbard, eating his usual low-calorie fare and surrounded, as usual, by his faithful circle of top managers, jokes that the station has no maternity policy.

"What?" asks a visitor. "Did you ask Cyndy to leave?"

"Leave?" echoes Hubbard in a shocked voice. "Leave? Hell, we wanted her to have the damn baby on the air! Can you imagine the publicity?"

Kaki Tuohy, the programming director and only woman in Hubbard's elite, grins as she reaches for a cracker. "Another first," she says. "Another Hubbard Broadcasting first."

"Damn right, another first," says Hubbard emphatically—but he doesn't smile.

"Hubbard" and "first" are two words this man doesn't take lightly. To his mind, they belong together, as they have been throughout the career of his eighty-four-year-old father, Stanley Eugene Hubbard, who lays claim to Minnesota's first amateur radio set in 1912; the first plane-to-plane radio contact in his days as a pioneer aviator; the first commercial radio station in Minnesota in 1923; the first radio news service anywhere, begun

41

between Chicago and St. Paul when United Press International refused to serve the then-infant radio industry; the first NBC television affiliate; the first television station in the Upper Midwest and the third in the nation when KSTP-TV began broadcasting in 1948. The list goes on—first station to go all-color, first station to broadcast news regularly—a KSTP litany of firsts.

Stanley Stube Hubbard, the son, has kept his father's traditions. KSTP is one of ABC's most-watched affiliates, and the two Hubbards may be, in another sense, the cities' most-watched broadcasters. As well known as the rotund blue "5" that KSTP plasters across the cities' billboards are the antics and passions of these two mavericks: their hatred of unions, their love of zoos, their ferocious devotion to news, the son's fanatical attention to hockey, their mutual infatuation with all things technical, the wizardry of all things television. "We had the first color-film processor of any station," says Harold Meier, a news director in the early days of television. "We had the second one ever made— I think NASA had the first." The son has a weather department equipped with twenty-three weather observers, one jet helicopter, nine meteorologists, Doppler radar, and no fixed budget. "If we need it, we get it," says George Merrill, KSTP's chief engineer. In Minnesota, where weather is a serious subject, the U.S. Weather Service calls KSTP for tips.

Famous, too, are their right-wing politics and their hands-on approach to running KSTP— "with a fist in every pot," as Skip Loescher, an ex-employee who successfully battled the Hubbards in court, puts it. Nobody at the CBS affiliate, WCCO, their rival for the past five decades, gets this kind of attention. "But I don't know if anyone here *wants* that kind of attention," says Jim Rupp, a WCCO executive.

Though you wouldn't know it to look at its ratings, KSTP is also the last of a dying breed: the family-held, family-run station, whose founder, at eighty-four, still presides as chairman of the board. Five grandchildren work at the station when they're not in school. "It's a family business," says Hubbard. "We talk over everything. We have forever."

With jug ears, receding blond hair, and eyebrows so light as to be nonexistent, Stanley S. Hubbard, at forty-eight, looks like a startled six-year-old. He's got the energy of a Cub Scout troop on its first outing—and some of the same mentality. "I'm not for Carter," he announces, loping down the halls of KSTP, "I'm not for Reagan. I'm for *freedom.*" A tiny flag flies in his lapel, its patriotism corny but real.

Hubbard's conversation is an odd mixture of evasiveness and point-blank directness. "He's, for me, the living definition of arbitrary and capricious," says one former employee. "He'll keep people guessing, he always keeps people off the point. He doesn't like anything that's formal or prepared—he wants to think he cuts through all that stuff." He can be unnervingly frank and profane, exploding his opinions with all the forethought of a kid throwing a firecracker.

He doesn't drink, doesn't smoke, sleeps like a baby, and displays a magnanimity as unexpected as it is genuine. Fired employees stay on the payroll until they find another job; chemical dependency treatment for employees is confidential and free. "He presents many sides," says that same ex-employee. "You'll hear about some really nice things he does, and you'll hear about some really bad things—and they'll both be true."

Stanley E. Hubbard, for reasons unknown to the rest of us, did not give his son his own middle name. He did, however, bequeath to him Hubbard Broadcasting, a corporation whose holdings, worth upwards of $200 million, now include a luxury hotel, a marine electronics supply company, a remote-unit television production company, a sixty-six-foot yacht, and, most pertinently, three television stations and five related radio stations: KSTP-TV, AM, and FM in St. Paul, Minnesota; WTOG-TV, a UHF independent in Tampa-St. Petersburg, Florida; WGTO-AM in Cypress Gardens, Florida; and KOB-TV, AM, and FM in Albuquerque, New Mexico, an NBC affiliate.

And the Hubbards may have another first to add to their list. Like them, it is both simple and shrewd, defensive and daring. They call it the United States Satellite Broadcasting Company Inc. (USSB). Stanley E. Hubbard is its chairman, his son its president and *raison d'être*. USSB is the younger Hubbard's response to a perceived threat: the direct-broadcast satellite, or DBS.

Latest noodles in the alphabet soup of the New Television, swimming alongside CATV, HDTV, and LPTV, DBS should be distinguished from FSS—fixed-service satellites. Those are the broadcast satellites that currently send signals to public television stations and to the nations's 2,000 cable systems, carrying such now-familiar pay-television fare as uninterrupted movies, sports events, and Ted Turner's superstation.

Perhaps as many as ten thousand people have gone to the trouble and expense ($5,000 or more) of erecting in their yards an unsightly umbrella-shaped dish, ten to fifteen feet in diameter, to pirate these signals from the sky. Imagine the appeal of a dish about the size of a saucer a kid might use to slide down a snowy hill, which you could charge at your neighborhood Sears for a few hundred dollars and carry home under your arm. That's all you'd need to pick up a DBS signal, which is stronger and on a higher frequency than the FSS signal.

DBS systems may rain as many as forty new channels of television down on the land by the end of this decade. How does DBS threaten people like Hubbard? It doesn't, necessarily. It could bring more television to the places already doing a booming business in the larger earth stations—remote areas that get few or no conventional television channels. And it could bring multi-channel pay television to people living in the 30 to 40 percent of the nation that will probably never be wired for cable.

On the other hand, DBS can also provide the most direct method yet for getting a television signal into a home. It is television without the middleman—without stations like KSTP to relay programs, and without broadcasters like Stan Hubbard.

"I'd been thinking about DBS for a long time," says Hubbard, speaking from his wood-panelled office in the Hubbard Broadcasting building, "and I, like every other broadcaster, was worried about it." His thinking was jolted when the FCC agreed to consider a 1,132-page opus from Comsat, the nation's largest satellite manufacturer, proposing several satellites to cover the United States with three to five channels of pay television. In considering Comsat's proposal, the FCC opened the door to proposals from competing systems.

"That's when I really started thinking about it," Hubbard says. "Struggling in the back of my mind was: How the hell do you merge the concept of DBS and the concept of the local broadcaster? And, all of a sudden, like a light out of the clear blue, it came to me that it would be possible to do it."

He came up with another Hubbard first—a DBS system of his own. His scheme could remove him and other local broadcasters from the middleman's role and put them in a position to benefit from DBS: He could form a confederation of local stations, build a system of direct-broadcast satellites, program the system with the help of his confederation, and beam channels directly to anyone with a dish.

Hubbard's DBS application arrived at the FCC only a few weeks after Comsat's. In it he proposed a system of two large satellites, each with two beams, or "footprints." Each beam, carrying three television channels, would cover one U.S. time zone. The first channel would carry general-audience entertainment programming very much like network fare—sitcoms, serials, soap operas, talk shows, news, and last but far from least, advertising. The second would be a twenty-four-hour all-news channel, programmed to a large degree by the news departments of the local-station confederation, in a kind of Associated Press of the sky, and the third would be left open for some unseen future development.

In each USSB market, one independent station—or network affiliate, if no independent wanted to join and an affiliate could be wooed away—would get exclusive rights to rebroadcast Hubbard's material. As the networks do now, he'd compensate them for whatever share they cared to rebroadcast—regardless of how many dishes were getting the programming in their area—and stations could cut in with their own local news, other programs, and local advertising. The programming would come, in part, from the same Hollywood studios that bless us with their output on the Big Three now—Lorimar, MTM, and Norman Lear—and also from the new production facilities Hubbard plans to build in St. Petersburg and Albuquerque.

The application promises great things for localism, most of them through the wonders of satellite technology. The stations in the top fifty markets would be required to install an "uplink" to transmit signals to the satellite. Their signals would then go, on a weaker beam, to a master feeder in the Midwest, which would either record them or send them back up to be rebroadcast by other systems—nationally or regionally.

Not incidentally, many of the larger independent stations already have satellite uplinks. "Nothing Hubbard's suggesting can't be done," says Steve Bell, general manager of the Los Angeles independent, KTLA, which has been beaming its "Richard Simmons Show" nationwide with spectacular success. "It's all being done right now." For example, "Independent Network News," which airs across the country during prime time, uses local stories from a host of independent stations every night. Hubbard's plan would give local stations regular satellite time and encourage them to relay their own productions as often as possible; a similar approach at PBS has engendered some of its most innovative programming. Unlike PBS, though, Hubbard would compensate local stations for their contributions.

As a final inducement to join, Hubbard would give member stations first crack at a public stock offering of nonvoting shares (Hubbards, elder and younger, will control the voting stock). And they'll elect a board, with its own full-time executive, to oversee the operation of the system. "Grassroots input," the application calls it; a system "truly national and local at the same time."

Beyond the limits of the independents' signals, and in towns where there is no independent station, Hubbard would offer rebroadcasting rights to low-power television stations (LPTV). Only one such station happens to be operating at the moment—from Bemidji, Minnesota—but when the FCC approves the thousands of applications pending, these stations, with their ten-to-fifteen-mile range, should spring up like mushrooms after a Minnesota rain.

One could almost accuse Hubbard of overkill. His plan uses every non-network television outlet to be had: the independents, the low-power stations, the dishes—and, theoretically, the cable systems that would have to rebroadcast the independents' signal. There would be duplication in the programming that reaches the home, but to what extent no one can be sure, until these small dishes are actually in the marketplace competing with cable and conventional television. And the USSB signal would provide different fare to different people: Those with dishes would get USSB's local and regional programming only from a satellite; those with conventional sets would get their local programming from a station, as well as whatever that station chose of local and regional programming from USSB's satellite, and those with both (whew) could take their pick.

"The idea," Hubbard says. "is to have a DBS system *and* maintain the strength of the local broadcaster. With our plan, the local station is, number one, a news bureau, number two, a producer, and number three, a carrier of any part of our programming. If he does less over the air, he'll still have income from the other two.

"Yes, we're becoming [our own] competition," he continues, a note of exasperation creeping into his voice at having to explain the obvious. "We have to. The question is—are you going to sit and let the world pass you by, or are you going to move ahead and be part of the future? You can't have it both ways."

If Hubbard is guilty of overkill, it may be because he has to be. No RCA or Comsat, able to bleed for years until DBS becomes profitable, Hubbard needs a national audience right from the start so that he can sell national advertising—$786 million worth the first year of operation alone. The networks, with access to 98 percent of American homes and more than 200 affiliates each, bring in more than a billion dollars in advertising a year each, and they've been at this a long time.

As far as Hubbard's concerned, advertising is more than a necessity, it's a downright virtue. Free, over-the-air broadcasting is what made this country's television great, he believes. Free television—the kind the Hubbards make their money from—will sustain USSB. "People like ads," he says. "We have some research to prove it. They think it's a small price to pay for the programming."

Hubbard's DBS application is in a lot of company. The FCC had expected perhaps one or two applicants besides Comsat. It got fourteen, including one from two inmates at an Indiana state penitentiary. After weeding these out, the agency took eight proposals and a portion of a ninth for serious consideration.

Hubbard made first cuts. So, too, did RCA, CBS, Western Union, and Comsat. The size of these corporations reflected the vast sums needed to put a DBS system into operation. Hubbard's, not surprisingly, was one of the least expensive, proposing $300 million for satellite costs and nearly a billion dollars for the first year of operation. Aside from the $786 million in advertising, funding would come from underwriters, partners, and banks. In the first year, the lion's share of the costs—$647 million—would go to programming. That's considerably less than the networks allot for programming now.

Most of the other applications were based on some combination of pay and advertiser-supported television. Two companies, RCA and Western Union, proposed that their satellites be common carriers—provided they retain the option to choose their clients. Direct Broadcast Satellite Company, another early entrant, wanted to lease varied amounts of satellite time to any and all takers. And CBS wanted to preempt all the others by reserving the entire spectrum in question for high-definition television, a new process creating a clearer television image by doubling the number of lines on the screen.

For all the variety in these proposals, they all ignored the traditional local broadcaster—the middleman. All of them, that is, but Hubbard's.

Back in Minnesota, the snow falls on another winter, another hockey season begins, and Stan Hubbard checks over the bid for the state high-school hockey tournament, which his KSTP covers with eleven cameras and three "slo-mo's," roughly the allotment ABC gives a game on "Monday Night Football." Hubbard's love of hockey has become something of a local joke. Though paintings on every wall of his office testify to his love of sailing, it's Hubbard's passion for hockey that gets attention—probably because he once preempted a nationally televised NCAA basketball game to show a St. Paul semiprofessional hockey team, the Vulcans. He did it, Hubbard says, to help his television crew bone up for the hockey tournament, but the presence of his oldest son, Stanley Eugene, Jr., on the rink in a Vulcans uniform created a furor that still lingers in local memory.

On another plane, though, Hubbard's devotion to this most vicious and chaotic of team sports is an apt one for a broadcaster in such times as these. "Hockey was very important to me psychologically," Hubbard once told a sports magazine. "Football and baseball are completely structured sports. Hockey is the only game where a nonconformist can find himself."

A lone headline tacked on Hubbard's wall reads: "Stanley Gets Praised and Blamed." So, too, does his brainchild, USSB. "Anyone who looks at Stan Hubbard's proposal and doesn't take it seriously just has his head buried in the sand," avows Ron Sherman, president of the entertainment division of J. Walter Thompson, amending an initial negative response from the ad agency quoted in *The Wall Street Journal*.

But bleak prognoses come from media analysts in Manhattan. "The function of affiliates to distribute programming is an obsolete one," declares Anthony M. Hoffman, an oft-quoted entertainment analyst with A.G. Becker. Hoffman believes Hubbard is deliberately ignoring the role of cable in the years ahead. "Unfortunately, he's inventing a fourth network." Hubbard Broadcasting's ability to sustain the losses in operating USSB raises Hoffman's doubts. "I think Hubbard's also invented a new concept of profit and loss."

"I will personally eat my way to Minneapolis from New York if Stan Hubbard gets one-tenth of the advertising numbers he projects for the first year," corroborates Stanley Moger, a New York syndicator and president of SFM Entertainment. "The advertisers are not going to take $300 million from each network and place it in a nonentity. I say, yes, it's a viable idea, but not at those figures." Moger knows Hubbard personally. "I think there's a lot of ego involved here," he says, "but I wish him well, I really do. I would love to be proven wrong."

Independent stations have taken a wait-and-see attitude toward the plan that Hubbard arranges so flatteringly around them. "I can see where a lot of the low-power stations might need his service more than we do," says one independent manager. Another, Hal Protter of KPLR in St. Louis, is chairman of the new technology committee for the Association of Independent Television Stations (INTV). He's so convinced of the merits of the idea that he's already flown to Minneapolis with his boss, Ted Koplar, to investigate. Herman Land, president and a founder of INTV, expresses a more cautious view. "Any really serious comment is premature," he says. "Ultimately, of course, it's the programming that counts. It's all well and good to have a good structure, but it's what you put into it that will make or break the thing."

Hubbard counts 182 independent stations as potential members of USSB, but to tap the growing strength of independent stations in any significant way, he'll need to persuade the twenty stations in the top thirty markets to join. Two vice presidents of Hubbard's new corporation are recent refugees from important independent stations—James Coppersmith, from New York's WNEW, and Robert Fransen, from the Minneapolis competition at WTCN. They're expected to draw on their personal connections among the independents, which the Hubbards, as lifelong network affiliates, don't have.

The maverick Hubbards have been network affiliates for many years—but not with just one network. After a thirty-five-year association with NBC, Stan Hubbard startled the industry in 1978 by joining forces with ABC, then on the ascent and wooing new affiliates. Hubbard impressed the industry with his timing and nerve. But his decision was more practical than brave: It was in part for ABC's promise of translator stations, which would make KSTP a more powerful station than it had been with NBC.

Hubbard's reputation as a maverick didn't hurt him in this instance. ABC filed against DBS, but casts a benign eye on its favored adopted son. Says Robert Fountain, the ABC vice president who engineered the Hubbard courtship, "We're as impressed with this as we were with them before. It's no less than we would expect." And Donald Swartz, president of the Minneapolis station that lost its ABC franchise to KSTP and has since become the most-watched station in the independents' top twenty, feels the same way. "Sure, he's a maverick. But sometimes it's the maverick who comes out on top." Hubbard, by the way, has no intention of switching yet again to make KSTP an independent flagship for USSB. In fact, he's already offered that slot to Swartz—who is considering it.

No one has ever accused a Hubbard of being subtle. They've never been a part of the Twin Cities elite—the Daytons and the Pillsburys and the newspaper families who built the Guthrie Theater and Walker Art Center. No, Hubbards build hockey rinks. They outfit the St. Paul police department with its first car radios, and then S.E. Hubbard installs one in his own car, the better to call his station and get it to the scene of the crime before the cops.

They have a bloodhound's instinct for the neglected, the overlooked, the exploitable obvious. Join independent television stations, low-power television stations, saucer-sized dishes, and Hubbard Broadcasting, and you may not have the preservation of American localism. But you might very well have the preservation of Hubbard Broadcasting.

5.

The State of the Revolution 1982

Martin Koughan

History will record 1981 as the year American business gave financial substance to the Telecommunications Revolution and broke the ground for social change. The speculation and blue-sky analyses finally gave way to concrete business strategies, as some of the nation's largest corporations plunged billions of dollars into mammoth new communications projects. Most of these ventures have won the blessings of the federal government, which looks hopefully to the developing technologies as keys to a revitalized economy.

These activities were scarcely noted outside the financial community, but their effects will be felt throughout the country, and even internationally, in the next few years.

To bring the state of the revolution into focus, we examine four developments emblematic of the trends for the eighties:
- The entry into cable by Piedmont Natural Gas, a North Carolina utility with annual revenues of $300 million;
- the partnership formed by ABC Inc. and Group W to provide two satellite news services;
- the publication by Sears Roebuck of a merchandise catalogue in a new medium, the optical video disc;
- the introduction by IBM of its first personal computer.

Although it may appear that these business efforts are shooting off in all directions—two-way cable, satellites, video discs, and computers—in fact they are all headed in a single direction: They all converge on the same instrument, the home television receiver. What this means is that the commonplace television set will play an even larger part in our lives by the end of the decade than it already does.

The revolution has been sparked by a series of ambitious business deals. It is indeed a supply-side phenomenon, powered less by consumer demand than by businesses that are intent on reaching consumers in a new way.

But two other dimensions—the interests of consumers, and those of the society generally—must be given at least equal attention. For the Telecommunications Revolution is not just going places, it is taking us with it.

Piedmont Natural Gas wanted to diversify into a new, unregulated business that would allow the company to build on thirty years' experience as the natural gas utility in Charlotte, North Carolina; it decided to go into cable television. If that strikes you as a curious choice, then you may not have realized, as the executives at Piedmont already have, that the utility and the communications businesses are rapidly becoming one and the same.

"It was a business that fit. Cable television is really a utility's business," claims John H. Maxheim, the company's aggressive young chief executive officer. Piedmont is the first regulated utility to win a cable franchise, and it almost certainly won't be the last. "We just want a little piece of the action. But anyone who wants in will have to get in very quickly."

This sense of urgency is quite new to the cable-television business, which after decades of sluggish growth has entered a period of almost frenzied development that will bring it into 60 percent of the nation's television households by the end of the decade. The fierce competition for control of the wire into the home signifies the business community's recognition that cable provides a new direct line to the American consumer, an electronic superhighway with immense commercial potential that will transform the humble television set into the most versatile, the most important, and probably the most expensive utility in the home.

"The new technologies, especially cable, will have a radical impact on our society," predicts Dr. George Gerbner, dean of Pennsylvania's Annenberg School of Communications. "What we are seeing is a shifting of the structure of investment and power. It is the new vehicle for extending capitalism in both reach and power."

Piedmont's diversification into cable was spearheaded by Maxheim, who was initially attracted by the "unbelievable cash flow" generated by such pay-entertainment services as Home Box Office. But the more he studied cable, the more similarities Maxheim saw to the gas business. Both require home installation, service, and a sophisticated computer capability. But cable's real utility function, Maxheim is convinced, stems from the new relationship between the consumer and the supplier of services that interactive systems make possible.

"Two-way cable is a tremendous opportunity," Maxheim says enthusiastically, "Cable television is going to go well beyond entertainment. I don't see any consumer service that cannot be delivered into the home over cable."

The services Maxheim envisions are made possible by a technology called "videotex," which allows the user to communicate with remote computers. The cable subscriber, using a simple keyboard terminal, will have at his disposal a dazzling array of new information services—continually updated news and weather, transportation schedules, educational programs, even electronic mail. But the most significant application of videotex will be transaction services such as home banking and "teleshopping."

Indeed, two-way cable holds promise as the ultimate energy saver by allowing routine business to be handled electronically, which will help consumers cut down on nonessential travel. But there are even more direct applications for an energy company, as the executives at Piedmont Natural Gas are learning from a test they are conducting jointly with American Telephone & Telegraph, the world's largest regulated utility, which already controls an interactive wire in most American homes and has its eye on the lucrative home-services market.

In March 1981, AT&T began a one-year, $6 million test of an electronic home energy management system in nearly a thousand Charlotte homes. Each customer received a small microprocessor connected to a modified Sony television set that displays the latest weather report, daily messages (such as warnings of power outages), and up-to-the minute energy usage figures. Participants can use the system to program major appliances, such as furnaces, water heaters, and air conditioners, to save money by operating in off-peak hours. All can be controlled remotely from any push-button telephone, allowing the customer, for example, to switch the air conditioner on at home before he leaves the office. AT&T estimates the system could cut home utility costs by 20 percent.

"The main motivation for the consumer is money. It gives him immediate, direct feedback—a way to control his destiny," says Eddie Stubbins of Duke Power, the local electric utility participating in the test. Some observers, however, question whether the consumer is the real beneficiary of such systems.

"There is an absolute gain for everyone, but the relative gain for those in control is a hundredfold," notes Annenberg's Gerbner. "Everyone will have a terminal, and that will provide the home with autonomy, but the central computer will have access to everyone and everything."

Energy management systems will save consumers money, but they will save utilities much more. Accomplished electronically, meter reading, billing, and collection are faster and more accurate, and can be done at a fraction of the present cost; to electric utilities the potential efficiencies are monumental. For the last two years, Duke Power has offered customers cash incentives for permitting the utility to install an interactive wire to major home appliances, which can then be shut down for short periods during peak demand emergencies. By 1990, this direct load management will eliminate the need for more than $10 billion in new plant construction, according to company estimates, since the system allows existing plants to be used more efficiently.

Many experts frankly doubt there will be enough consumer interest to support such videotex services. But what the skeptics fail to take into account is that service providers have a much larger stake than the consumer in making two-way services happen, and that they are likely to provide the economic incentives necessary to get the wire into the home.

"If we had to rely on the consumer to pay for all these services, they might never happen," says John Maxheim. "There are great advantages here on the supplier end. As more and more people get cable service, the suppliers will come on line—banks, retailers, and others—and they will subsidize the service because it's good business for them."

"Using the two-way wire, we can do just about anything we can dream up in the future," says Bill Lindner, Piedmont's vice president for technology. "For example, we could monitor consumption on a daily basis for theft. If there is a sudden drop in consumption, the computer could run up a red flag, and we could have a serviceman go to the home to see if the resident's bypassing the meter."

"What we will be doing is striking a Faustian bargain, where the Devil offers us all these good things at the cost of our souls," warns Dr. Joseph Weizenbaum, an MIT computer scientist concerned about the privacy implications of two-way cable. "When you put this together with other electronic monitoring opportunities, like home banking and burglar alarms, then it really does become possible to create a complete picture of what we are up to day and night.

"I'm sure it starts out benignly. Why worry about an anti-pilferage device? We don't pilfer. But clearly there is the opportunity here for surveillance on a colossal scale. We may be cementing things into place that, if we thought about it, we may not want at all."

There are no federal statutes currently governing the use of information collected by two-way cable, and protections written into local franchise agreements are few. With deregulation such a byword today, most legislators seem to agree with Piedmont's Maxheim that "regulations mean approvals, and approvals mean delays."

"You can't stop this thing, but you ought to have ground rules," declares Henry Geller, director of the Washington Center for Public Policy Research. "There should be the expectation of confidentiality. You should be able to know what information is being collected and have the right to access. But you have an indifferent public and a very militant industry. The pace of all this is very fast and very disturbing."

The Turner Broadcasting System began operating television's first twenty-four-hour news service in June 1980, and even though Cable News Network (CNN) charged cable operators fifteen cents a customer and sold advertising as well, it lost money at the rate of a million dollars a month. In the face of such losses, it is hard to imagine how a competitor could come along with two similar services, and offer them free of charge. If that does not seem crazy enough, consider the fact that the end of 1982 saw not one but three twenty-four-hour news channels.

The battle for control of cable news might seem slightly unreal—a complete suspension of conventional business rules. Yet it is only one skirmish in an escalating programming war that is literally out of this world—22,300 miles above the earth, in geostationary satellite orbit.

By the end of the decade, scores of program services will be raining down from satellites, providing cable viewers a cornucopia of choices for every imaginable taste. "Narrowcasting" — the targeting of programs to relatively small, specialized audiences—is accomplished using transponders, the satellite relay points that instantly transform a local station into a national network. The intense competition to serve these special audiences by satellite is good news for the consumer but risky business for the programmer.

"The fragmented audiences won't support all this programming," predicts media analyst John Reidy of the Wall Street firm of Drexel Burnham Lambert. "More money will be lost on programming for cable TV in the next five years than will be made in the next ten."

CNN is the brainchild of flamboyant cable entrepreneur Ted Turner, one of the first to recognize the potential of satellite distribution. In 1975, a transponder on RCA's Satcom I (now Satcom IIIR) turned his Atlanta, Georgia, UHF station into superstation WTBS. With a national audience of 17 million and revenues of $50 million, it boasts being the largest television service after the three commercial networks.

The challenge to CNN comes from the very people who denounced Ted Turner's superstation maneuver—two of the nation's largest broadcasting operations, Group W (Westinghouse Broadcasting) and ABC News. Undeterred by CNN's dismal bottom line, the new partnership will actually pay cable operators to carry its two Satellite News Channels, a move that has prompted Turner to invest, grudgingly, $15 million in a second twenty-four-hour service to match his competitors.

"What concerns me is who my competition is," says Turner. "The corporate colossi are on the way. The networks used to say this was crazy. Now they're killing to get in."

Broadcasters and the networks have dropped their once-determined opposition to cable with the encouragement of the present Federal Communications Commission, chaired by Reagan appointee Mark Fowler. The FCC strategy is to lift regulation in favor of open competition and to promote rapid development of new program sources—a policy that marks the beginning of a shift from the traditional concept of public airwaves to the pragmatic reality of private airwaves.

"With the Fowler approach to the marketplace, you'll see

more broadcasters in cable programming," says Dr. Roger Fransecky, public-affairs vice president for the Westinghouse cable division. "It takes tremendous capital resources and an in-place distribution system to compete. The companies with the most resources and the best positioning are going to win out. It's going to be a free-for-all."

Westinghouse took a major step toward achieving a strong position in the new marketplace by acquiring Teleprompter, the second largest multiple cable system operator (MSO) in cable. The largest merger of two communications companies in U.S. history, this move gives the programmers of Group W—backed by the enormous financial and technical resources of parent Westinghouse Electric—ready access to 1.5 million homes.

The speed and the scope of such transactions have many observers worried. "The vertical integration of cable-system owners controlling program suppliers has the effect of freezing others out of the marketplace," contends Sam Simon of the National Citizens Committee for Broadcasting (now Telecommunications Research and Action Center). "These companies are not competing, they're just integrating."

"Right now there are almost no independent satellite networks not owned by the big MSOs," claims Turner. "And the MSOs will not carry competing services."

Genuine competition in cable programming is being further stymied by a serious bottleneck in the cable pipeline. There are currently thirty-seven program services distributed by satellite, yet the oldest of the nation's cable systems still have only a twelve-channel capacity. Until they are rebuilt—and until cable's penetration improves on the current 27 percent—satellite programmers face lean times. Only those with enough resources to withstand several years of red ink—such as Westinghouse and ABC—are likely to survive.

Yet even programmers willing to take their chances in this marketplace will have trouble finding a transponder. Although satellite capacity will triple by 1984, virtually every transponder now contemplated is already reserved.

While Westinghouse was buying Teleprompter, it was also making a deal with Western Union to secure ten transponders on the new Westar satellites, in an arrangement that has drawn a great deal of fire.

"Westinghouse is warehousing transponders," charges Sam Simon. "They don't have any reasonable need for the quantity they are buying."

Others question Western Union's right to make such a deal in the first place. The Robert Wold Company, a firm that subleases transponder time to cable and broadcast programmers, was the first company to use a satellite for a television broadcast. Wold, one of Western Union's oldest customers, had a standing order for additional transponders and expected to receive the next one available. But the explosive demand for transponders has prompted many satellite operators to ignore their federally mandated common-carrier obligation to lease access on a first-come, first-served basis; instead they have been selling transponders to the highest bidder. When Westinghouse entered the picture, Wold lost out. Along with others, he has petitioned the FCC to enforce its common-carrier rules. Western Union declined to comment on the matter, explaining that it was in litigation.

According to Wold, these new practices could knock the small entrepreneur out of the satellite business. "As you turn from leasing to selling, you begin to rule out the small operator purely on the basis of economics," he says. "You now need $8 million to $18 million to be considered for a transponder."

"Give the market five years to operate like this, and how many ultimate sources of programming do you imagine there will be?" asks Don Ward, Wold's attorney.

New means of distributing program services—notably direct-broadcast satellites (DBS) and low-power television stations—are expected to open up by the middle of the decade. But DBS requires investments in the billions of dollars, and low-power stations, with a broadcast range of only ten to twenty miles, could have difficulty attracting the audience and advertisers needed to survive.

"The biggest lie in this whole thing is the claim that the marketplace will insure diversity," says Sam Simon, whose organization has filed thirty applications for low-power stations. "We have a situation where corporations are controlling the pipeline—its content and our access to it. Would we allow AT&T to decide what is said over the telephone, or who can or cannot get one, based on economics? The issue is not that these companies abuse the power, it is that they *have* this power."

"The fight has focused on the economic stakes and not on the public-policy questions," observes Fred Wertheimer, president of Common Cause. "Leaving it to a battle of the Titans is not the way public policy should be framed."

"As long as you are not absolutely free to get into the business, there is scarcity and the government must protect my interests," says public-interest advocate Everett Parker of the United Church of Christ. "Those who can pay will get access, but if they try to monopolize it, it will bring a big outcry for hard-line regulation. This is the time when these companies should be exhibiting some enlightened self-interest. They could turn out to be their own worst enemies."

Sears Roebuck and Company made its mark on retailing in the 1880s when it introduced its now-famous catalogue and began selling directly to consumers in their homes. Today, the company is preparing for the future by returning to its roots: Sears' marketing strategy for the twenty-first century anticipates a gradual return to the nation's living rooms.

A special edition of this year's summer catalogue provided an early indication of where the Goliath of American retailers is heading. Shoppers at test stores in Cincinnati and Washington who turned to the new catalogue's fashion "page" were greeted with waves crashing onto a beach as models strolled across the sand to musical accompaniment. Cheryl Tiegs then introduced herself and her signature line of sportswear, explaining why Sears means value to the consumer.

Called Tele-Shop, this unusual catalogue was assembled on a laser video disc manufactured by DiscoVision Associates, a partnership of IBM and MCA, the entertainment conglomerate. Thanks to the disc's random-access feature, customers were able in less than three seconds to summon up both still-frame and film sequences vividly describing—with sight, sound, and motion—any one of 18,000 products.

"We think the laser video disc is the ultimate marketing tool available today," says Ronald Ramseyer, national manager of Sears' catalogue advertising. "The key advantage is the possibility of getting to consumers [with] content that is more exciting, more interesting, and more persuasive than print. From ninety-five years of selling experience, we know that when you can show a product in living, breathing color, there is a direct relation to sales."

The laser video disc combines the imagery and immediacy of television with the flexibility of a printed catalogue, making it possible to "sell at each customer's persuasion level," as Ramseyer puts it. But Tele-Shop is more than just a better catalogue; the experiment is part of a long-term strategy based on the company's recognition that consumer shopping habits are changing. Growth in the number of single households and working couples with limited discretionary time has caused mail-order sales to increase twice as rapidly as other retail sales have. This trend toward home shopping has prompted Sears to look to interactive cable as an ideal electronic pipeline for delivering video catalogues.

"The two-way dimension is vitally important," says Ramseyer. "Seventy percent of our catalogue sales are conducted over the phone, which is, of course, two-way communication." Sears will eventually be able to link a battery of video discs to the central computers of interactive cable systems. By using videotex, any subscriber would then be able to request complete video presentations for specific products, which could be ordered by pressing a button.

Teleshopping could account for as much as $250 billion in retail sales by 1990, but perhaps even more significant, it will provide the manufacturers of consumer products the most accurate information ever available on what motivates the customer to buy. The distinctive feature of cable is that it permits the targeting of individual households within a television market, a potential that market researchers have already begun to exploit. Behaviorscan, one technique now in use, enlists test groups of cabled homes to receive specially tailored television commercials. Each participant receives an identity card to present at the checkout counter of the local supermarket. Grocery purchases are then "scanned" by a low-power laser beam and fed into a central computer, enabling researchers to study the connection between what consumers saw on television and what they actually bought.

"The effect of this on market research will be similar to the effect the invention of the telescope had on astronomy," declares John Keon, marketing professor at New York University. "For the first time, we can measure action—the impact of persuasion on consumers."

"Behaviorscan allows us to go through a community household by household and decide what ad we want the consumer to see," explains John Malec, chief executive of Information Resources Inc., the company that invented the technique. "It has already changed an advertiser's ability to identify high-potential markets right down to the zip-code level. The only thing lacking to get to that level is the delivery system."

Two-way cable will not only provide that delivery system, it will transform the moment of persuasion into the point of sale, a development with profound implications both for advertising and consumer buying habits. "Advertisers will get better and better at selling because they will know their customers better and better. One effect will be an increase in impulse buying," predicts Keon. "You will have ads designed to make up your mind very quickly. They will have a high emotional content. I can imagine the smoke-detector ads you might see."

But commercials for consumer products are not the only form of advertising likely to change with the advent of two-way cable. Politicians already rely on television to sell their candidacies to the public, and interactive cable will offer the candidate an even more powerful new tool that could effect fundamental changes in our political system.

"Following that electronic path into the home has staggering implications whether you are marketing dog food or a political candidate," observes Harry Shooshan, former chief counsel of the House Communications Subcommittee. "In a city that is heavily cabled, a media consultant could pick a channel and tailor his message to highlight certain issues and avoid other issues completely. A spot on abortion, for example, could be sent only to Catholic homes. It may lead to more efficient and effective campaigning, but it will not result in a more informed electorate. People who are being told what they are likely to want to hear are not better-informed."

Perhaps even more disturbing is the possibility that two-way cable will tempt elected officials to submit difficult policy questions to an electronic referendum. "I fear in that kind of system that policy could be made by whim," says former FCC chairman Charles Ferris. "You have to slow down and listen in our republican form of government. It is a slow, reflective process. It's good for a leader to stay in tune with his constituency, but there is an obligation to provide leadership and judgment. If one overemphasizes the electronic referendum, you will have a dramatic change in the way our government works, and I think that's frightening.

"There will be some situations where the marketplace won't protect us," admits Ferris, who promoted the deregulation of the new technologies during his tenure as FCC chairman. "What should we do to safeguard the democratic process? I just don't have an answer. Maybe someone should be concerned about it."

International Business Machines has always been something of a corporate snob. The $26 billion colossus has cornered nearly half the world computer market with the business philosophy of building only the biggest and most powerful business computers and selling them exclusively through its own sales force. That's why to many observers, this year's most significant business event was the introduction of the IBM Personal Computer, a typewriter-sized machine that will be available at Sears and other retail outlets.

"IBM going into the consumer market says the home-computer market is really here," concludes Robert Schrank, a specialist in computer technology for the Ford Foundation. "It will make the computer as common as the calculator. When Radio Shack introduces a personal computer, it's cute. When IBM does it, it's for real."

The home-computer market promises to be one of the most explosive new businesses of the eighties, and with the arrival of the best known and most respected name in computers on the scene, the home information revolution could shift into high gear. To the astonishment of veteran IBM-watchers, the company's basic $1,565 model uses the standard television set for its display screen, and will perform such mundane tasks as storing recipes and playing video games. But IBM's first consumer electronics product is no toy.

"The IBM Personal Computer is the functional equivalent of the giant computers of the sixties that cost a couple of million dollars," says MIT's Joseph Weizenbaum. "They are essentially equivalent in power, except that the personal computer is much faster."

By bringing such awesome power to the fingertips of the television viewer, the personal computer will become the nerve center of the home information system, and it will provide a solution to one of the most troubling questions posed by the Telecommunications Revolution: How will consumers keep up with the information explosion? The personal computer, as editor and television programmer, will be able to select, from the torrent of information and entertainment that will surge into cabled homes, those items particularly interesting to the viewer. It can perform this gatekeeper function because the personal computer will be programmed to know more about the individual user's tastes and interests than any human would have the patience to learn.

By the end of this decade, you might begin your day reading and watching an individually tailored news report prepared by your personal computer from dozens of print and broadcast sources coming in over the two-way wire. The report would highlight developments related to your business and personal interests. (If you were planning a vacation to Mexico, for instance, it would include up-to-date information on the country's weather and the exchange rate. You could also request the computer to order your airline tickets and hotel reservations.) The news report would be followed by a daily personal schedule that might, in its course, alert you to a discrepancy on a finance charge that your computer uncovered overnight while it was communicating with your bank's computer. Then your computer would connect with the one at your office to check for any calls and messages. Before getting ready to leave for work, you might instruct the personal computer to prepare an analysis of new automobiles, including financing and insurance information, with a recommendation on the model that would most economically meet your needs. Finally you could request a rudimentary Spanish lesson (for the trip to Mexico), to follow the night's schedule of entertainment, which the computer would select and record during the day. This scenario might sound like science fiction, but all these functions and more are well within the capability of the personal computer.

"The home-computer revolution is at least equal in importance to the invention of the printing press and the Industrial Revolution," claims Dr. J.F. Traub, chairman of the computer science department at Columbia University. "It will provide unlimited access to information, and information is power. Eventually, personal computers will be ubiquitous, like the telephone and the automobile."

Many observers do not share Traub's optimism, arguing that today's consumers will probably not be willing to embrace such sophisticated technology. But this argument fails to take into account the enthusiasm of one influential group that has no fear of technology. Known as the "on-line generation," they are the youngsters who while away hours hypnotized by the genius of electronic games, who spend their summers designing complex programs at "computer camp," and who play with computers in elementary school the way their parents played with crayons. These computer kids will be the personal computer's best salesmen, and when they themselves become consumers, they are the group most likely to exploit the full potential of the new media.

The on-line generation is learning a revolutionary new way of thinking and communicating, which will mean that the children of the eighties will possess an electronic literacy beyond the experience and comprehension of most of their parents. This technological generation gap may present the family with one of its most serious challenges. Yet this is only one of the potential schisms that could result from the Telecommunications Revolution—it may also drive yet another technological wedge between the rich and the poor.

"Social problems stem from inequality of distribution," notes Dean Gerbner of the Annenberg School. "Technology never solves social problems, it extends them to different depths. Those who have the most, who own the machines, will get the most out of rapidly expanding sources of information. The more we centralize our cultural and informational resources, the more we risk widening the gap between the information-rich and the information-poor."

"All of these new technologies cost money," observes Nolan Bowie, the former director of the Citizens Communications Center. "The First Amendment says that people have a right to communicate, to receive information. In the present situation, you will get as much First Amendment right as you can afford. Technological literacy is involved here. The rich schools will be teaching their kids computer, but the inner-city schools are having a problem with basic reading comprehension. The lowest economic class can barely read, never mind use a computer."

Access to the new technologies will also be limited by factors other than age and economics. "For the completely interactive telecommunications system, only the big cities will work," predicts Stephen Effros, a lawyer who represents small cable-system operators. "In small cities, two-way cable will be totally uneconomic. The rural-urban schism has existed for years in terms of schools, hospitals, and other facilities. It will deepen with the new communications services."

Effros is a former FCC attorney who works out of his suburban Washington home using a personal computer; the experience has led him to wonder if the liberation provided by the new technologies might not also isolate us. "If my personal computer focuses on one area, and your personal computer focuses on something else, we will only see what we want to see. We will know nothing about anything else. The information explosion could turn out to be an information *implosion,* where we all focus too narrowly. We will be experts and idiots at the same time."

Since 1950, television has served as the main vehicle of the nation's mass culture, the source of information and ideas common to us all. But as the new technologies spread, and the mass-television experience becomes a more personal dialogue, something important may be lost. "Television is a mass ritual," says Dr. Gerbner. "It provides interaction for people who have little in common and has brought everyone into a huge mainstream. It is not an entirely negative phenomenon. The mass ritual is a window on the world, and that is a need and a desire that the new machines won't satisfy. The big question is whether the new technologies will replace and impoverish the mass ritual."

"Whatever this thing is, it is a social experiment on an extremely grand scale," claims computer scientist Weizenbaum. "Technology will not only allow you to enjoy luxuries, it may become a membership card required to function at all in society. What happens to those who don't participate? The differences between those out and those in will be much sharper in the future, and migrating from one group to the other will be more difficult. It is possible that we will have a society split apart, in a permanent state of civil war."

Today's synergism of two-way cable, satellites, laser video discs, and personal computers will mean a quantum advance in human communications. But with all the exciting new opportunities for business and for the consumer will come a host of new problems and challenges. Television's radical transformation will in turn transform us.

"One of the fascinating things about television," observes Fred Wertheimer, "is that we tend to think we're conscious of the effect it's having. But we have never been as conscious as we should have been about TV's effect on our lives. We have all along missed the implications of the role it has played. And we are about to do it again."

6.

Are the Networks Dinosaurs?

Les Brown

I t has been a neat, efficient sort of business: three networks pumping out programs and advertising for hundreds of local stations and millions of consumers. No running to the newsstand, no waiting in line for tickets. Bang—television is right there in the home, produced, distributed, and displayed instantaneously.

A beautiful business: three networks in one vast sellers' market, with a captive audience worth billions of dollars. The advertisers line up for air-time. Best damned selling tool ever devised.

But the heartbeat of commercial television has not been the advertising or the programming, it has been the audience: people seeking diversion, or a mental anesthetic, or to be in touch somehow with the outside world; people who habitually go out into the neon-lit electronic village where CBS, ABC, and NBC are the main streets. Unlike all other entertainment and informational media—books, movies, concerts, plays—television has not had to generate its audience. The viewers have simply been there, ahead of the programs, in predictable numbers every hour of the day, growing to a hundred million people at the peak of an evening. The networks' main challenge has been in dividing up the audience, since the network that gets the largest piece of the captive market can charge the most for advertising time. One year NBC ran a poor third and still made record profits. Quite a business—sweet and failure-proof.

And that's the way it has been.

But in the new world of television it is the present, not the past, that is prologue, and the present is a mighty tide of change. If some people have difficulty getting a firm sense of the present, it is surely because they confuse it with the future they have heard about for so many years. This is indeed the old future that was to bring a communications revolution, and now it is doing its work.

The present finds cable penetrating close to 30 percent of American households, with most of the largest population centers still untapped. In Pittsburgh, Warner Amex recently christened the country's first eighty-channel cable installation, signaling what's to come in the wiring of the cities; the system, moreover, is interactive. The cable systems existing today have, on average, signed up only half the households on the streets they've wired, which means that overnight—given the right impetus—the 30 percent national penetration could grow to 50 percent or even more.

If ABC, CBS, and NBC are the main thoroughfares of the electronic village, cable has claimed the side streets. Some forty-seven new networks are in the sky riding satellites that beam down on cable systems. Each of them is pursuing a segment of the television audience, some with movies, sports, or news, and others with services the networks have largely ignored—rock music, the arts, education. Few of these networks are profitable businesses yet, but that hasn't deterred entrepreneurs from seeking satellite space for still more cable services, even at the going rate of $13 million for a satellite transponder.

The object for now is to stake a claim on the continually expanding cable frontier, perchance to strike some equivalent of oil, gold, or natural gas, as Time Inc. has already done with its pay-cable network, Home Box Office, the most potent rival yet to the commercial networks.

Meanwhile, STV—or over-the-air subscription television on UHF channels—is flourishing in urban areas not yet invaded by cable. Video games, the precursors to home computers, have captured the fancy and leisure time of millions of young people. The market for home video appurtenances—video recorders, video-disc players, video cameras—is moderately lively, and there is always the possibility that elements will come together (as happened with rock, FM radio, and home stereo) to make it a booming market.

The revolution turns on people paying for television; it follows logically that viewers willing to pay will seek to get their money's worth. What makes everything different for the broadcast networks today is that the old sellers' market, on which they thrived for some thirty-five years and which allowed them to take viewership for granted, is rapidly becoming, and will remain, a buyers' market.

The evidence is already clear. Viewers with pay cable watch more television than those without it. On certain nights, Home Box Office is the leading network in the ratings in households with pay cable. Overall, the networks' share of the market is declining, although in total numbers the audience count remains approximately the same because of population growth.

Nielsen statistics for prime time reveal a dramatic shift: For the fourth quarter of 1979, ABC, CBS, and NBC together attracted 92.1 percent of the viewers in the peak hours; a year later that fell to 88.2 percent, and for the same period in 1981 to 84.8 percent. For the entire 1980-81 season, the networks' combined share was 81 percent, and there is no reason to suppose the downward trend has been halted in the season just ended.

In Columbus, Ohio, in homes equipped with Qube, Warner Amex's two-way cable system, the networks' prime-time share is only 70 percent. And in Wilkes-Barre, Pennyslvania, one of the birthplaces of cable, the networks' share is already down to 60 percent.

Independent stations, many of them sending programming by satellite to cable systems, and most of them receiving programs by satellite, are making larger claims on the network audience.

And on the near horizon are direct-broadcast satellites, videotex, and low-power television.

Like the powerful forms of life in prehistoric times, the networks find themselves in a radically changing environment—with viewers liberated from their thrall, new contenders chasing the advertising dollar, technologies emerging that change the nature of the viewing experience. The dinosaurs vanished because they couldn't adapt to the physical and climatic changes on the planet. There is good reason to wonder whether the networks can adapt to the harsh conditions of the new electronic age.

Gene F. Jankowski, who as president of the CBS Broadcast Group sits atop one of the most powerful communications organizations in the world, has fielded the dark question of the networks' survival before. He likes the analogy to main streets. "Be assured," he declares, "CBS will still be one of the main streets in 1990. The doomsayers have it wrong. The burden to compete and survive is not with the established networks but with the new ones. You can't ignore the differences of scale—our size, experience, and financial strength against theirs. This isn't to say there won't be changes in the next few years, but we'll still have the lion's share of audience and advertising in 1990."

Then what are we to make of CBS's partnership with Twentieth Century-Fox in new video ventures? Is CBS laying the groundwork for survival in the new age?

No, it isn't a survival measure, Jankowski replies. "We have as much reason as any other company to take advantage of the new opportunities. Much of the time, more than half the homes in the country are not watching television. Obviously, some markets are not being served well."

Jankowski speaks of big television and little television. Big television is the networks. In 1981 they were being watched in 38.8 million homes on a typical evening, while the various pay-cable networks were tuned in by 1.6 million. The CBS network alone averaged 14.3 million homes per minute during the year, while the highest-rated advertising-supported cable service, Ted Turner's superstation, WTBS, averaged fewer than half a million.

"We shouldn't underestimate the power of the network system, or the difficulty of competing with it head-on," Jankowski says. In his view, the strength of the network system derives from three structural concepts: weekly series, to make the most of popularity; nightly schedules, which viewers carry around in their heads like the map of a neighborhood; and local station affiliations, through which national and local services are directly linked. He considers the relationships with affiliates "the backbone of the system."

The CBS vision of the future is one of plenty for all. The company projects an expansion in the number of television households from the present 80.4 million to 99 million by the decade's end, and also foresees continued growth in hours of television usage: a larger pie for big television and little television to share. According to the CBS forecast, in 1990 the networks will have combined revenues of $15 billion, pay-cable $5.4 billion, and advertising-supported cable networks $2 billion.

ABC is also bullish on the future, and more aggressive than the other networks in entering new markets that compete with commercial television. "It's not that we're hedging our bets, but keeping stride with the times," explains Herbert Granath, president of ABC Video, the division created for the new communications enterprises.

A joint venture with Hearst Corporation, known as Hearst/ABC Video Services, has spawned two cable networks—ARTS, a cultural service, and Daytime, which provides a block of women's programming based on magazines of the Hearst group. In another partnership, with Group W Satellite Communications, ABC is revving up two cable news networks that will compete with the two established by Ted Turner. In addition, it has teamed with Getty Oil's cable sports network, ESPN, to deal in pay-television sports events. And as CBS had done, ABC has formed a motion-picture production unit to turn out this mainstay of pay-cable and commercial-television programming. ABC Video announced a plan to provide pay-television service during the middle of the night to people with home video recorders. And it began yet another partnership—this time with Cox Cable for the development of pay-cable hardware and software. Granath hints of more ventures to come.

In its latest annual report to shareholders, ABC presents itself as a communications (rather than broadcast) corporation and provides this view of the future:

"Broadcast TV networks and stations will certainly share the largest audiences. If they have 75 percent of the audience in 1990, just 25 percent remains for everyone else (even if the broadcast share were only 60 percent, 40 percent would remain [sic]). But competitors for that remainder already number in the dozens, and may eventually total a hundred or more."

Why would ABC invest so heavily in cable services if the competition is going to be so fierce and the shares of audience so small?

Because, explains the annual report, advertisers will pay a lot more to reach sharply defined audiences on cable networks than they pay for the large, amorphous audience the networks deliver—as much as three times more, by ABC's reckoning. Therefore a small audience can produce a fair profit. And that also holds true for pay-cable enterprises, where a 1 percent share of the audience can be a bonanza when it consists of sports fans paying $15 for a single event.

So two networks are positioning themselves for any eventuality in the new world of television and have the financial resources to go exploring. But what of NBC, the third player in the network game? It has been running such a miserable third in the ratings race, and so far out of the money, that it can scarcely think about entering the age of Television II. All its energies are focused on scrambling out of the Nielsen depths.

"The way we look at it, we're in a growth industry just staying in broadcasting," says M.S. Rukeyser, Jr., the official spokesman for the National Broadcasting Company. "You realize it's a terrific business when you consider that Chrysler would have gone under if what happened to us had happened to them. Even with our terrible slump we didn't lose money last year. We made about $30 million. Sure, the other networks made ten times as much, but that just shows what our potential is for growth. We're still in the same medium they're in and playing to the same audience. If ABC could come from way behind, why couldn't we?"

The answer may be that ABC made its surge in a rapidly expanding commercial-television market. It grew in boom times, with a lot of luck. It was helped, for example, by the Prime Time Access Rule, which reduced network schedules to three hours a night; by the death of the old star system (high-paid, big-name celebrities, then considered necessary to the success of a series, wouldn't go near ABC); by the popularity of the 1976 Olympics; and by the creation of the Family Viewing Hour, which caused all three networks to shake up their prime-time lineups. The circumstances are quite different today. NBC is mired in third place and attempting its climb when audiences are falling away from commercial television and program prices are rising. The advertising money that used to support three networks may dwindle to supporting two-and-a-half networks. In the seventies ABC had only two competitors, and even a third-place network could not be desperately weak in a sellers' market. In a buyers' market, however, the bottom is all the way down.

The optimistic forecasts of CBS and ABC are probably correct, so far as they go. The explosion of channels by itself poses no devastating threat to the networks in this decade. ABC, CBS, and NBC are still the centers of popular programming, and their penetration of households is almost five times that of the leading cable network. Commercial television promises to continue commanding the heaviest viewing for a good while.

But the network forecasts are based on the assumption that no further significant changes are occurring in the electronic environment, and that's where their picture gets distorted. They omit the technology that will have the greatest impact on the network system: the communications satellite. For if cable is creating a buyers' market for the television consumer, the satellite will create a buyers' market for the local television station. And that is bound to alter the relationship Gene Jankowski calls "the backbone of the system," so vital to the networks' strength, and indeed to their survival.

People tend to think of the television networks as three giant broadcast organizations in New York. In reality, they are webs of stations carrying a common television signal all across America. For more than thirty years these webs have been made of telephone land lines. The networks send out the signal over the lines, each to some two-hundred local affiliates, which transmit it on the airwaves. The networks pay the affiliates for their air-time and provide them with glamorous, attractive programming. It is significant that no independent (unaffiliated) television station has ever been the leader in its market.

That was once also the case in radio; network affiliates were the aristocracy. But with the changes occurring in listening habits during the early sixties, radio stations suddenly found it advantageous not to carry network programming. Important groups such as Westinghouse Broadcasting Company severed all their network affiliations. Radio networks dried up into little more than purveyors of news on the hour.

That could also happen in television—and even in this decade. The satellite, a new kind of delivery system, liberates stations from their dependency on ABC, CBS, or NBC, making all manner of small, ad hoc networks feasible. A television producer like Norman Lear, for instance, could bypass the networks and deliver his series directly to the stations, in effect creating his own part-time network.

The gains in audience made by independent stations during the last few years have coincided with their satellite-receiving capability. Most independents have dishes allowing them to bring in network-like programs, such as "Independent Network News" and "Entertainment Tonight." "The Merv Griffin Show," which used to be syndicated by the traditional method of shipping tapes from station to station, now goes out by satellite and airs in many cities just as if it were a network show. Each station carries each episode the same day.

Having switched in 1978 from land lines to satellite interconnection, the Public Broadcasting Service provides the paradigm for a television-by-satellite system. During much of the broadcast day, a public television station will receive two, and sometimes three, streams of programming simultaneously from the satellite. In any time period, it selects from the options the program it will air.

Applied to commercial television, such a system would give local television stations a choice between programs scheduled by the network and any other offered by independent distributors. While the networks would seem to have the inside track at the stations, outside distributors could gain the time periods they want simply by paying the stations more than the networks do for their airtime.

Since the networks are merely middlemen between stations and program suppliers, they could actually be eliminated if the Hollywood studios should decide to deal direct. Lorimar, for example, would have little trouble lining up two-hundred stations to carry "Dallas" and advertisers to buy the spots. This way, production companies could realize the full financial benefit of a hit. Under the existing system, the studios lease their programs to the networks for a set fee and don't share in the bounty if the program turns into a blockbuster that makes the advertising rates soar. This has been a sore point in the students' relations with the networks.

The only thing preventing program producers today from circumventing the networks is the stations' slowness to invest in satellite receiving dishes. As soon as there are enough of them to cover the country, television will change radically as a business.

So the networks are faced at some point with becoming providers of programs to stations, rather than the full-time conduits they have been. What the networks produce themselves is mainly news and sports programming, which is one reason they are striving to expand their evening newscasts, and one reason the three networks together just spent an unprecedented $2 billion to secure the National Football League rights for five more years.

But even as they struggle to immunize themselves against technological change, the networks have developed organic ailments that can only weaken their resistance. Rising programming costs have upset their economic system. In order to cope with soaring inflation, the networks have increased the number of commercial spots in prime time, which is hardly the shrewdest way to regain robust health, since larger doses of advertising are bound to displease viewers, affiliates, and advertisers alike.

There is talk now in network circles of finding cheaper ways to develop television series. Co-productions with foreign television companies, scoffed at before, have begun to make sense. So have increases in news and prime-time soap opera programming, as those forms generally cost less than episodic entertainment series.

Even with one network faltering in the competition, the other two are in a sweat to keep profits up. (It only adds to the current panic that, despite huge expenditures for program development, the networks last season came up with the fewest new hits ever in prime time.) The conventional networks' great advantage over any cable network has always been that they do not rely on a wire to enter the home; their signals can move both over the air and through the wire. But even that advantage is fading. Several network affiliates have already begun contracting with cable satellite services to carry some of their programming. Every station in America now knows that, if it chooses, it can substitute the Cable News Network or the Satellite News Channel for the ABC, NBC, or CBS newscast. Affiliate loyalty, the networks are learning, is nothing to count on in a buyers' market.

Evidence is accumulating that the old business of network television—the business webs, affiliates, and nightly schedules—is inexorably in decline. The old business, that beautiful business, is the dinosaur. The companies we call the networks, however, are well equipped to survive and flourish in the new environment—two of them, at least.

It is already hard to discuss the networks collectively in the old way, as triplets in a lock step. Each is on a separate course—or, we might say, in a different stage of evolution. NBC remains implanted in Television I, the old network business, probably to its peril. CBS cautiously straddles the line between the first age and Television II. ABC is venturing boldly over the new frontier, covering all routes to the television set.

If only because they have the running start, the networks may well remain the leading forces in Television II. They also have glamour, know-how, and financial resources. When the present network system gives out because of its dependency on affiliated stations, ABC, CBS, and even NBC could conceivably preserve themselves as networks by feeding programming via satellite to a nation of cable channels. Their options in the new world are as unlimited as anyone else's.

7.

America's Global Information Empire

Herbert Schiller

A new international economic order is being created rapidly, unobtrusively, and, in this country at least, almost without journalistic attention. Dependent on the global flow of information and fueled by advances in communications technology, the development is encouraged by business and government leaders in the United States because they believe it carries hope for a revitalized economy. The emerging new alignment finds its justification and chief support in a single phrase that expresses a distinctly American idea: the free flow of information.

But America's enthusiasm is not shared by many other countries, particularly those of the Third World. They view the movement of data across borders—and the technologies that facilitate it—with concern and alarm. In their perception, the so-called Information Age enjoyed by the developed nations represents a new kind of domination.

This story goes largely unreported in America, where the growth of an information-based economy is good news for business, and where the rhetoric of free flow is as difficult to oppose as the First Amendment. Yet it is a story that may well come to haunt this country in the years ahead, for it will significantly shape our relationship with the rest of the world.

A growing number of countries are beginning to fear that

America's use of the free-flow doctrine—to encourage television broadcasting from satellites, transborder data flows by giant private corporations, and satellite photography of the earth—will do little to enhance their economic independence; instead, these countries suspect it may be a strategy for further subjugating their interests to those of the wealthy countries controlling the development and use of the new technologies.

The roots of this colossal perceptual disagreement between America and much of the rest of the world lie in the old mercantile system, which the new economic order would replace. For the ascendancy of information industries is the direct result of the expansion of U.S. manufacturing business abroad. Lured by foreign markets, raw materials, cheap labor, complacent governments, tax havens, and tariff exemptions, hundreds of American corporations have developed foreign holdings whose total value now exceeds $200 billion. (This sum represents American-owned plants and equipment, whose productive capacity is larger than the national outputs of all but three or four countries.)

With their operations scattered across the globe, these companies depend on sophisticated communications technologies (often linking computers and satellites) to provide them with the constant flow of information they need to run efficiently. The information encompasses everything from their investments, production schedules, pricing, wages, and raw-material inventories to currency-exchange rates, taxes, advertising, and legal decisions.

Although these technologies are most commonly used to increase the efficiency of traditional manufacturing industries (especially those located far from corporate headquarters), there is growing expectation that information processing and transmission will become a dominant industry in itself. As Vincent Giuliano, senior analyst for the consulting firm Arthur D. Little, has written, "A small but increasingly powerful group of decision makers—in government as well as in industry—is now coming to believe that an ideal way to relate to the world economy is as an idea and knowledge exporter, based on sophisticated tools." Similarly, John Eger, who directed the Nixon Administration's White House Office of Telecommunications Policy and is now a vice president at CBS, has urged that America win "the international information war" through a combination of government support for the information industry and a willingness to accept the demise of "sunset" industries—the older, industrial sectors of the economy.

Indeed, many companies whose products are used for electronic communications are experiencing a boom: in the manufacture of satellite microchips, computers, and thousands of related electronic items. Demand is also growing for computer software, database organizers and assemblers, data processing, and data transmitting. Most recently, super corporate combines have begun to appear. These giants use the new technologies to integrate many previously separate services under one roof—as Sears has done by offering its customers not only retail services, but also banking, real-estate, insurance, and stock transactions.

All this makes the information industries seem a good bet for reviving the U.S. economy and insuring the continued growth of U.S. businesses abroad. If that prospect is appealing, the political rhetoric behind it— "the free flow of information" —sounds even better. It *seems* to stand for freedom and against censorship. It is meant to protect not only the information on which industry depends, but also information not directly related to manufacturing: movies and news services, television programs, banking transactions, access to computer data services—almost anything, in fact, that can be communicated by words, numbers, or pictures.

Why then are so many countries threatened by a doctrine that sounds like a noble corollary of political freedom? The reasons have to do with the history of our international economic relations—especially those with the Third World.

While much of American foreign investment is concentrated in industrialized regions such as Western Europe, Canada, and Australia, a significant portion of foreign holdings lies in less developed regions of Asia, Latin America, and Africa, where American investments have created new manufacturing enclaves for turning raw materials into processed goods. By and large, the sites have remained under the direction of the transnational companies that control their operations. Wages are low, and the foreign-owned corporations traditionally take most profits out of the country for investment elsewhere.

The resentments and hostility engendered by this system gradually gave rise to demands for a new and more equitable economic order—one in which the developing countries would get a better deal for their raw materials as well as a bigger say in their own economic development. But if the United States has its way, the new world economy will be based on the very technologies whose explosive growth facilitated the rapid expansion of American business abroad—technologies instrumental in creating the unequal economic relationships that poor countries seek to rectify.

U.S. government support for the emerging information industries has taken more concrete—and disturbing—forms than the simple advocacy of a free flow of information. Many of the new technologies, especially communications satellites and computers, were made possible by forty years of colossal expenditures on military research and development. And in fact, beyond their role in the corporate world, these technologies provide the control mechanism for global American military security. Many countries see the development of the new information technologies as little more than the direct result of America's quest for worldwide commercial and military advantage.

The combination of dramatic changes in the domestic American economy and the increasing reliance of U.S. businesses abroad on information technologies has given the "free flow of information" doctrine a new importance. For half a century, the doctrine was a favorite of diverse media interests—news agencies, film and television producers, publishers, and record companies—which campaigned regularly against any foreign laws that might restrict the exportation of their products. The doctrine was the most effective rhetorical instrument for prying open markets (often cornered by Europeans) in the name of human rights and individual freedom.

When the Associated Press tried to oust Reuters from its long-held news markets in 1944, *The Economist* commented tartly, "Kent Cooper [the AP's executive director], like most big business executives, experiences a peculiar moral glow in finding that his idea of freedom coincides with his commercial advantage.... Democracy does not necessarily mean making the world safe for the AP."

As *The Economist* noted, the free flow of information was no more than a convenient rationale serving business's interests. Today, it is just as much a myth as it was in 1944. The flow of information within and among societies isn't free at all; it is still shaped and controlled by the powerful interests that can afford the necessary technologies. (The only questions are, who are they, and whom do they represent?) But something important has changed since the 1940s: The free-flow doctrine has become essential to the evolving economic system, both at home and abroad.

Consider an IBM executive's recent remarks before a congressional subcommittee: "IBM does business in more than 120 countries . . . We are, therefore, very dependent on a free flow of information in order to maintain our operations worldwide . . . to communicate worldwide engineering, design, and manufacturing information . . . to move financial and operational information among our various organizations as freely as possible. Finally, we must interact continuously with international banking and transportation facilities, such as airlines, which, in turn, also depend on a free flow of information to conduct their operations."

Hugh Donaghue, vice president of Control Data Corporation, is more blunt: ". . . the basis for new management is a growing dependency on the free flow of information, and consequently, a growing vulnerability if the free flow is restricted or stopped completely." Within this context, it is easy to see why the free-flow doctrine has been elevated to the highest levels of foreign policy. Philip H. Power, owner and chairman of Suburban Communications Corporation, has stressed that attacks on the free-flow doctrine would imperil much more than media interests alone: "The stakes in the coming battle go far beyond editors and publishers. . . . They extend to the great computer- and information-hardware companies whose foreign sales of billions of dollars are at stake; to the TV networks and movie makers whose entertainment products range the globe; to the airlines and banks and financial institutions whose need for computer-to-computer data literally defines their business; to the multimillion dollar international advertising industry. . . ."

To poor countries, such statements as these suggest not only that the new information industries will revive the U.S. economy, but that they will also attempt to guarantee future U.S. dominance in the world economy. The developing nations thus fear that the new economic order will merely substitute a new dependency for an old one: Instead of providing cheap raw materials to make manufactured goods they can barely afford to buy, poor nations could wind up supplying cheap raw data to make high-priced processed information.

Already, the United States imports more data than any other country; it is also the world's largest exporter of processed data. Against this background, the free flow of information takes on a more insidious meaning.

Nowhere is this more evident than with developments in remote sensing satellites. These remarkable devices study land masses and oceans in minute detail. They can reveal crop conditions, mineral and fuel location, fish concentrations in the seas, and geophysical data. If remote sensing were employed for the common good, it could clearly offer enormous benefits to all humankind. But that "if" is a very big one: Since their first use in 1972, remote sensing satellites have been devoted almost exclusively to corporate and military purposes. If U.S. industry leaders have their way, they'll continue to control the operation of the satellites. Frederick Henderson, president of the GEOSAT Committee, echoed a common sentiment when he told a congressional subcommittee in 1979, "The United States cannot afford to lose the remaining advantages that have come from developing techniques that have allowed us to become primary finders and developers of the world's nonrenewable resources." Given the limits of the earth's bounty and the struggle for control of scarce resources, this is no small matter.

Indeed, remote sensing satellites are currently in the vanguard of America's attempt to forge new pathways for the free flow of information. This attempt denies the people whose territories have been "sensed" —even without their request or permission—the right to claim sovereignty over information concerning their own natural resources.

Several years ago, Dr. Irwin Pikus of the State Department's Environmental and Scientific Affairs Bureau told a congressional committee that "many developing countries guard their natural resources quite jealously and are considerably concerned that advanced countries might be able to exploit them." Once information and data are in the hands of others, argued Pikus, the developing countries have no claim on sovereignty: "We do not consider the question of sovereignty negotiable."

United States policy-makers extend this less-than-accommodating perspective to other forms of international information flow. For instance, direct broadcasting from communication satellites into home receivers is also considered an inviolable right of the transmitting party (against which the receiving public has no legal recourse).

More important to the corporate economy, so are transborder data flows—the electronic information moving silently across frontiers over computer and telecommunications circuits. Any attempts by foreign countries to regulate the flow of information across their borders are regarded as interference with the "free flow of information." Thus the basic requirements and interests of U.S. business are colliding more and more often with those of developing nations, as well as those of competing developed economies.

But despite growing international opposition to the free-flow doctrine, U.S. government and business leaders continue asserting their First Amendment right to free speech—and insisting on its international applicability and judicial appropriateness.

This tactic is doubly mischievous. By conferring on billion-dollar private combines the right of the individual to free speech, the government is weakening legitimate concern for genuine individual liberties. And its attempt to impose American laws and institutions on other countries encourages chauvinism abroad and at home.

Even our customarily friendly Canadian neighbors have complained that the real issue is not the "freeness" of information flow but jobs and national sovereignty. An official Canadian commission studying the implications of telecommunications for Canadian sovereignty recently warned that "greater use of foreign, mainly U.S., computing services, and growing dependence on them, will . . . facilitate the attempts of the government of the United States to make laws applicable outside U.S. territory."

Third World leaders have been even more forceful in their criticism of U.S. telecommunications policy. Africa, Asia, and Latin America are the most likely places for the imposition of a new international economic and information order—but it will be a very different system from the one they've been demanding for years. Emphasizing high technology, the emerging system ignores the need for fundamental changes that could make the world economy more egalitarian.

Understandably, many Third World countries regard the new information technology with great ambivalence. Satellites and advanced information processing could provide to developing countries invaluable information about the extent and location of their natural resources. Yet the transnational corporate system's stranglehold over the new technologies makes many Third World countries question who would really control the information. Still suffering from one kind of dependency, they are wary of risking a new one—this time based on information and information technology.

Their policies reflect their fears: In the United Nations, Third World countries have consistently voted against the United States doctrine of "free flow." They have been particularly agitated by American insistence that countries have no right to reject any communication-satellite signal—no right of "prior consent." The United States stands practically alone in its denial of this right.

Many issues vital to international communications are still to be decided: the allocation of orbital slots for communication satellites; radio spectrum frequency allocations; transborder data-flow rules, and the prior-consent issue itself. The rights of mammoth private corporations to operate internationally, heedless of and unaccountable to national oversight, are increasingly being disputed.

In 1980, the U.S. government issued a report that explained just why other countries opposed the U.S. information policy:

Whatever the particular perspective of a country, an increasing number of nations worry that the loss of control over information about internal functions can jeopardize their sovereignty and leave them open to possible disruptions ranging from uncontrollable technical failures to political sabotage.

The media haven't publicized the government's finding. In fact, they have paid scant attention to stories about information policies that in many instances will have direct consequences for their own future. The main providers of our daily news participate in and benefit directly from the arrangements and institutional structures they (sometimes) describe and analyze. Fairness and comprehensiveness can hardly thrive when such a monumental conflict of interest exists.

The danger is that without change, our government will continue to pursue policies favoring corporations that seek profits from the control and selective sale of increasingly vast stores of information. And these policies will be justified as furthering a "free flow of information" that will benefit us all. Our greatest need today may be to challenge *not* the enticing doctrines that invoke imperishable human and individual rights, but the misapplication of these desirable principles in the service of corporate and propertied interests.

8.

Subliminal Politics in the Evening News

Walter Karp

At the White House, Lyndon Johnson used to keep three television sets going at once so he could watch what all three network news programs were telling the voters about him. The late president, however, left no known record of his opinion of "NBC Nightly News," "CBS Evening News," and what ABC now calls "World News Tonight." This is unfortunate because it might have provided an answer to a question that exceedingly few Americans are in a position to answer, although some 33 million of us watch network news nightly. The question, simply, is this: Do the three network news shows differ politically from each other, and if so, in what ways? Or are all three, perhaps, just mass-media blurs?

It is not a question you can answer by rapidly twisting the dial back and forth. I tried that once; all you *will* get is a blur. Nor can you answer the question by watching a different network's news on different nights. The only way to discover differences is to see how each network treats the same day's world supply of note-worthy events. Even a video-cassette recorder alone will not do the trick. It only gives you two network shows: the one you watch and the one you record. You also need access to a public television station that broadcasts, as a service to the deaf, a late-night captioned rerun of the ABC news. Equipped with a recorder (rented), access to ABC reruns, and an invincible addiction to American politics, I sat myself down some days before the 1981 military takeover in Poland to keep running tabs on what most people casually refer to as "the seven o'clock news."

As the three-headed man, figuratively speaking, the first thing I discovered was an intriguing bit of secret knowledge. On any given evening, the network news shows often differ quite sharply from one another, even about major matters. One evening a few weeks before Christmas 1981, for example, CBS offered as its economic news in "this season of recession," a cheery report on price cutting in Chicago department stores. "A bonanza of bargains," chirped the CBS reporter. "The best Christmas present possible" for sufferers from inflation. That same night, NBC's economic news was "The Farm Squeeze," a grim account of hard times for America's small-farm owners, who were being ground down between low commodity prices and mountainous fuel bills. As for ABC, that same night it drew a dramatic contrast between President Reagan's political triumphs in the spring and economic conditions in the winter.

The very next night, however, CBS cast off its rose-colored glasses and came out with a dark, factual account of the deepening recession. "The figures are grim." Since the figures concerned America's falling industrial production—released that day—it was more than a little surprising to discover minutes later that NBC, the previous night's champion of the poor farmer, passed over the figures as if they were scarcely of consequence. ABC fell somewhere in between.

Then there was the president's last press conference of 1981, which took place on December 17. ABC and CBS treated it briefly and uncritically. NBC took an altogether different tack. Toward the end of the program it offered a remarkably severe attack on the president's performance. According to NBC News, he had been evasive and dishonest. He had made a grossly false denial in claiming that he had never promised to balance the budget—NBC showed footage in which the promise was made. He had made an equally false accusation in blaming the press for exaggerating the menace of the evanescing "Libyan hit squad," when, as NBC noted, all the drumbeating had begun at the White House.

In their treatment of the president that evening, the contrast between NBC and its two rivals could not have been sharper—at least for that day. Was NBC anti-Reagan? If so, what was one to make of NBC News on the day when the stock market dropped 17.22 points and Detroit produced its most catastrophic sales figures in a generation? If there was ever a chance to slam Reaganomics, that evening provided it. CBS, which had swallowed whole Reagan's Libyan menace story, plunged into the grim news with a vengeance. "The Agony of Detroit" was the title of its detailed account of America's worst economic disaster area. NBC thought otherwise. Its chief auto industry story was a feature about American cars being safer in a collision than Japanese models. Buy American, as they used to say in the age of Eisenhower.

All these nightly contrasts, I must admit, had me thoroughly baffled for a while. The differences did not seem to add up to any consistent political line. Moreover, each network seemed to differ from one evening to the next quite as much as it differed from its rivals. It took me some time to realize that the inconsistencies of a given network news program merely blurred—deliberately, I suspect—the edges of each network's quite distinctive political character. The blurs began to fade, however, as the network shows began coping with the stunning events in Poland and with the administration's reaction to them.

The swift imposition of martial law by the Polish army occurred on Saturday, December 12, which gave the network news programs (and myself) some time to consider what was at stake. Since the Reagan Administration, taken by surprise, was almost speechless for days, the massive influence of the White House did not fall at once on the media. They were quite free for a time to follow their own bent. What I intended to look for was the networks' handling of two facts that seemed almost self-evident. First, the Polish crisis threatened no American interest. It was a crisis—and a grave one—for the Soviet Union, which regards a subjugated Communist Poland as the keystone of its security. This fact the administration tacitly recognized when it later held the Soviets responsible, quite correctly, for the Polish crackdown.

The second fact followed from the first. Any serious American attempt to champion an independent Poland, whether in the name of Solidarity, liberty, or human rights, could have only one political end: to reduce the power and undermine the security of the Soviet Union. It would become yet another round in the imperious struggle with Russia for global supremacy, in other words, the Cold War. The situation in Poland was a critical moment for the U.S.S.R., a Cold War opportunity for the U.S., and a profound tragedy for the Polish people.

Since almost anything to do with America's thirty-five-year-long rivalry with Russia almost invariably gets distorted in the American press, it was with considerable trepidation that I waited for the story of the Polish crackdown to unfold on the three networks.

"CBS Evening News" at once confirmed my worst fears. In an ominous tone worthy of a Soviet invasion of Western Europe, CBS described the menacing "Soviet-backed Polish army" and its harsh repressions; played up unsubstantiated rumors of bloodshed, brutality, and heavy resistance; virtually concealed from its viewers the astonishing news that Solidarity had apparently collapsed in a trice. The next evening confirmed my sense of CBS's political object. It continued to report as fact any rumor that might arouse popular anger and raise up a cry for American action— "a wave of sit-down strikes" broken by tanks; troops rebelling against their martial-law masters; "Soviet officials working closely" with the Polish junta. In a fervent sermonette delivered a few days later, Bill Moyers (of whom more later) assailed the Reagan Administration for doing nothing to help Poland regain its liberties. Fresh from frothing over the Libyan menace, CBS seemed determined to further the cause of American intervention in Polish affairs.

When the administration eventually decided to champion liberty in Poland by imposing economic sanctions, CBS News began covering the Polish crisis as if it chiefly feared that its viewers would fail to support the president's initiative with sufficient fervor. It generally played down Allied criticism of the Reagan sanctions and the Polish Catholic Church's fear of their consequences. On the day a British reporter asked Secretary of State Alexander Haig the deadly question, namely why the United States was such a determined foe of military dictatorship in Poland when it aided and abetted military dictatorships elsewhere (from Chile to South Korea), CBS alone failed to feature Haig's fulminating incapacity to supply a convincing answer.

On Tuesday, December 14, when CBS News began whipping its viewers into a Cold War lather, I took it for granted that the network was merely reflecting the national revival of Cold War attitudes and assumptions. I expected the other two network shows to sound like CBS. To my genuine amazement, NBC that night (and thereafter) treated the Polish news with notable calm and detachment. That cosmopolitanism that treats every event in the modern world as if it were happening three blocks from the

White House was utterly absent from the NBC view. Instead of reporting inflammatory rumors, it noted at once that solid information about Poland was lacking. It cited, as CBS did not, a White House spokesman who termed the Polish crackdown an "internal matter." Just what NBC's detachment signified I was unable to grasp at once. On the one hand, it was an unspoken assertion of the fact that Poland did not touch upon America's security and consequently was not something to get dangerously excited about. On the other hand, it could merely have reflected NBC's adherence to the Administration's initial view of the situation.

ABC News proved even more surprising. Like NBC, it was calm, detached, and skeptical of rumors. It surpassed NBC, however, in the sharpness of its analysis of the Polish situation. Unlike its two rivals, it seemed to be genuinely interested in Polish politics. It was the first to note, for example, that the Polish army was not a tool of the discredited Communist Party, but in fact had swept it aside in what was, for all practical purposes, a seizure of power, the first military takeover to occur in the Soviet Union's European empire.

As for America's role, ABC, on December 16, made a particularly penetrating observation. It pointed out that the Reagan Administration seemed to fear that the U.S.S.R. would crush Solidarity, the politically insurgent trade union, without having to intervene directly. The implication was obvious: The Reagan Administration would have liked to see the crackdown fail, and thereby compel the Russians to engage in a costly and enormously damaging military invasion of Poland.

This, however, proved to be ABC's high point. At the president's December 17 press conference (the one that NBC lambasted), Reagan made it plain that the United States would soon commit itself to ending martial law in Poland through the use of economic weapons. America was about to become the official guardian of liberty in Poland after a thirty-five-year hiatus. Considering what it had reported on December 16, ABC might have noted just how questionable such a policy was. If the Soviet Union wanted Solidarity crushed, as the administration itself insisted, then a U.S. commitment to protecting Solidarity might well make invasion the ultimate outcome. America was skirting perilously close to combatting Russia with Polish lives. No such comment, or anything resembling it, came from ABC. By the time the administration had imposed sanctions on the Soviet Union—December 29—ABC was treating the Polish situation as if it somehow menaced America, a topsy-turvy view strongly espoused by Secretary Haig. But while CBS seemed to regard its viewers as untrustworthy "doves," ABC News showed no such fears. Its reporting on other aspects of Poland continued to be sharp, fair, and analytical as it tried hard to follow, for example, the tortuous political moves of the Polish Catholic Church.

Poland supplied me with a political score card: ABC and CBS seemed interventionist-minded; NBC did not. Indeed it was NBC's devotion to the tacit proposition that the Polish situation did not call for any serious American response that supplied the key to its quite precise political character. Despite the steady hardening of the administration line on Poland, NBC stuck to its last. On the day of the president's December 17 press conference, for example, it offered the results of a poll showing that 50 percent of the American people regarded the Polish crackdown as inevitable, meaning that half the country expected rebellious Soviet satellites to be squashed one way or the other. When the administration imposed sanctions against Poland on December 23, NBC alone emphasized that our European allies were sharply skeptical of the policy. NBC, too, was the only network to give a high Polish official time to attempt to justify the martial-law regime. On the other hand, NBC's report on the Marxist regime in Nicaragua was so hostile it verged on the inflammatory.

With that apparent contradiction, NBC's politics at last clicked into place. What its coverage of Poland reflected was not the attitude of post-Vietnam "doves," but something far stronger and more abiding in American politics. In its mild, upright way, NBC News still represented something of the old Midwestern "isolationism," with its aversion to overseas involvement combined with a highhanded attitude toward uppity Central American banana republics. The old isolationist sentiment, unrepresented now by either political party, cropped up in odd ways at NBC News. When winter storms buffeted America and Europe, for example, CBS duly reported the foul weather abroad. Not NBC. During the period I monitored the networks, it took for granted that snowdrifts in Britain held no interest whatever for its viewers.

Old-fashioned Midwestern Republicanism, upright, decent, and cautious; such was the political character of "NBC Nightly News," which, aptly enough, is the most popular network news show in the Middle West. The network's conservative treatment of economic affairs confirmed this in a dozen ways. The deepen-

ing recession NBC duly reported, but true to its political character, it concentrated on the sufferings of small-farm owners, small-
business men, and laid-off industrial workers rather than those of
the poor, the old, and the black victims of hard times. Moreover,
like most Republicans, NBC News seemed determined to give
Reagan's economic program "a chance"; it made no effort to link
the recession to Reagan's policies. In contrast, when the administration settled its American Telephone & Telegraph antitrust suit
out of court, NBC was far more critical of the terms than either
ABC or CBS, reflecting, I have no doubt, some surviving vestige
of the Middle West's once formidable hostility toward giant trusts
and monopolies. In a sense, "NBC Nightly News" was more
traditionally Republican than present-day Republican party leaders, a fact that was to give its treatment of President Reagan a
surprising and highly revealing turn.

There was no doubt where "CBS Evening News" stood on the
recession and Reaganomics. By mid-January its coverage of hard
times had grown powerful, persistent, and grimly eloquent.
Shadows of the Great Depression haunted CBS News: frightened
old people huddling at a hot meal center; poor children deprived
of school lunches; unemployed young men crowding soup kitch-
ens; victims of budget cuts; victims of hard times; victims of
Reagan. Unlike NBC, CBS made no bones of its conviction that
Reagan's economic policies were a failure, and a cruel failure at
that. Alarmist abroad, compassionate at home, CBS revealed a
political character as clear as NBC's. It represented, with considerable skill and *éclat,* the Cold War liberalism of the Democratic
Party—the party of Harry Truman and Dean Acheson, of "The
Great Society" and the Vietnam War, of Senator Daniel Patrick
Moynihan and the leaders of the AFL-CIO—hawks with a heart.
Since the liberal Cold Warriors are back in control of the Democratic Party, CBS News is virtually a party organ, unlike NBC,
which represents a political tradition far more than it represents a
party organization.

To embody so thoroughly a somewhat discredited political
party cannot be a happy situation for CBS News. This is where the
much-esteemed Bill Moyers comes in. Since beginning his CBS
commentaries last November, he has taken some of the Democratic Party onus off CBS News. Moyers delivers little sermons
whose general theme is that one pol is as bad as another, one
party as wretched as its rival, and that, taken all in all, American
politics is too repellent to think about. When President Reagan

began his campaign against leaks, he revealed once again the administration's extraordinary appetite for governmental secrecy, so sharply at odds with his continual attacks on governmental bureaucracy, which secrecy quite obviously protects. Instead of investigating that apparent contradiction, Moyers told CBS viewers that Lyndon Johnson was even more fanatical about leaks than Reagan. They're all alike, those bums. When it was revealed that Justice William Rehnquist, a conservative, had been temporarily deranged by medication and his condition concealed, Moyers chimed in with the reminder that the ill health of Justice William Douglas, a liberal, had also been concealed. After describing Reagan's economic program as one that may well lead to "collapse," Moyers concluded that the Democrats had nothing better to offer. That the Democrats have virtually disappeared as a political opposition is the beginning of an important political story. To use it as a getaway line is mere cynical posturing. Moyers' skepticism continually ended where serious political thought should begin. Yet there is method in this muddiness. If CBS News represents a tarnished party, it seem Moyers' function to pander to the cynical disgust that the Democrats' collusion with Reagan has engendered in the party's rank and file.

Given three networks and only two political parties, ABC, an upstart in the news field, has been forced to be something of a maverick, and an opportunist as well. Of the three networks, it is the least consistent from one day to the next. On the whole, however, it has cast its lot with Reagan and the Republican right, which probably goes far toward explaining its day-to-day variability, which included holding up Reagan's Libyan menace to scorn. Compared to the Democratic Party and to traditional Midwestern Republicanism, the Republican right provides a national network with a perilously narrow political base, and one that was not exactly growing larger in our recent winter of discontent. Despite the frequent surprises, ABC's right-wing character eventually comes through, if only because it is the only consistent thing about it. Like most of Reagan's right-wing supporters, for example, ABC News has expressed its disappointment with Reagan's foreign policy: Bellicose words have not been translated into bellicose deeds. He has offered "the rhetoric of a new foreign policy but not the substance," ABC noted in its critical summary of Reagan's first year in office. Alone among the three networks, ABC deplored Reagan's decision not to sell certain advanced fighter planes to Taiwan. "A bow to pressure from

Peking," ABC tartly noted, as if the ghost of the old China Lobby still haunted its purlieus, as indeed it still haunts the Republican right.

On domestic affairs, ABC generally (but not always) drew a mild picture of hard times and saw to it that Reagan's economic program was stoutly defended. On the day when the worst unemployment figures in recent history were published, ABC featured the president denouncing as a liar anyone who dared attribute the recession to any policy of his. When NBC accused the administration of backing off from antitrust enforcement—more shades of the old antimonopoly Middle West—ABC that same evening cited without demur the administration's lame denial that it had done any such thing.

In truth, the most revealing thing about ABC was how sharply it differed from NBC, the other nominally Republican news program, on certain fundamental points. One difference I already noted: ABC favors an assertive foreign policy, and NBC does not—a contrast reflecting the old isolationist/internationalist split that used to torment the Republican Party.

The second difference reveals something far more significant for contemporary American politics. The issue is Ronald Reagan himself. Although ABC does not treat the president as a sacred totem (it is protective but not reverent), it became clear after watching NBC News for several weeks that its old-fashioned Republicanism was deeply offended by the Republican president. ABC most certainly was not. NBC's criticism of the president's December news conference proved to be, in fact, the precursor to a personal indictment of Reagan that NBC began drawing up on January 14. The date is significant. It was two days after the political storm broke over Reagan's granting of tax-exempt status to two professedly racist colleges. That policy had angered a host of eminent Republicans, and so, quite possibly, it strengthened NBC's resolve to attack the president more boldly than it had done in the past.

NBC began with its account of the president's speech to worried business magnates in New York City. He "sounded more like a cheerleader than a chief executive," noted the NBC reporter, sounding the network's basic theme. On the same program, NBC—and NBC alone—offered a devastating example of the cruel mindlessness of Reagan's budget cuts: War veterans who die as paupers will no longer receive a free military funeral. Thanks to an administration that endlessly prates about patriotism, such veterans will be unceremoniously cremated, their ashes dumped in a common burial hole. American Legionnaires were "outraged," reported NBC News.

The next evening, NBC homed in on the Reaganites' determined hostility to the Freedom of Information Act, another reflection of the administration's appetite for secret government. According to a special NBC investigation, the administration's case for securing FBI immunity from the act is based on utterly false arguments. After the president's January 19 press conference, NBC News once again pounced on his lies, evasions, and misleading anecdotes. A few days later, NBC offered a telling example of the president's shortsighted frugality: A $40 million cut in the Coast Guard's budget was hampering its efforts to keep America's harbors safe for maritime commerce.

All in all, in the space of eleven days, NBC News had painted a devastating portrait of a president who lacked the very first requirement of a serious leader—an honest interest in the realities of the world. The network saw him, instead, as a man who wrapped himself in clichés, dogma, and self-delusion, ignoring as best he could the real business of the world.

I have dwelt on NBC's view of Reagan for two reasons: first, because it demonstrates that a network news program—a medium for the masses, for "ratings," for commerce—can be more politically courageous than the so-called leading newspapers of the country; second, and more important, because NBC's critical assessment of a Republican president strongly suggests that Ronald Reagan, dogmatic leader of a dogmatic faction, may well end up shattering his party. This is but another way of saying that the network news shows represent, with considerable fidelity, the active political forces in this country.

9.

The New Enemies of Journalism

Charles Kuralt

On the television news programs now, bells ring, pictures flip and tumble, and everybody seems to be shouting at me. This may be the way to do it, but I don't think so.

The news is bad enough without added jingle and flash. I think it would be better to tell it calmly, with as many of the details as possible, and not to try to make it more exciting than it is. I even think viewers would appreciate that, and tune in.

This runs contrary to the prevailing opinion at the networks. One of my bosses said of a program I used to work on, "We want to keep it a news broadcast, but one that is more interesting, rapidly paced, with more spontaneity and serendipity, almost like all-news radio. ... We want a news program that better serves the needs of people who don't have time to watch television for long periods ... and need to get information quickly."

I respect this man, but I respectfully disagree with his judgment. I don't see how a news broadcast can be quick without also being cheap and shallow. Almost any story worth mentioning is worth an additional word of explanation. The story told in a few seconds is almost always misleading. It would be better not to mention it at all. And all those electronic beeps and bells and flashy graphics designed to "grab" the viewer and speed the pace along only subtract a few more seconds that could be used to explain the events of the day in the English language.

The "quick news" idea has been preached for years by the shabby news consultants who have gone about peddling their bad advice to small television stations. They have never given a thought to the needs of the viewer, or to the reason the news is on the air in the first place—namely that this kind of country cannot work without an informed citizenry. The ninety-second news story does not serve the people; neither do the thirty- and twenty-second stories, and that's where we're headed. Fast. With bells and graphics.

In this sort of journalism there is something insulting to the viewer, the man or woman who sits down in front of the television set in the wistful hope of being informed. We are saying to this person, "You are a simpleton with a very short attention span," or, "You are too much in a hurry to care about the news anyway." Sooner or later, this viewer, who is *not* a simpleton and *not* too much in a hurry to care, will get the message and turn the dial. The networks are in a news-ratings race. The one that wins it will be the one that stays calm and intelligent and reliable—the most responsible, not the most excitable.

(I offer an analogy from the newspaper world: When I first came to work in New York, such sensational newspapers as the *Journal-American,* the *Mirror,* the *News,* and the *Post* nipped at the heels of the solid and reflective *New York Times.* The *News* is on its uppers, the *Post* is a joke, and the others are memories. The *Times* may be the only one of them all to survive.)

Even if I am wrong, even if it turns out that a network news department *can* achieve high ratings by putting red slashes on the screen and shouting out the headlines and jangling people's nerves, does that mean it *should?*

Right now, more Americans are out of work than at any time since the Great Depression. The president is asking that the country spend more dollars on military hardware than the government possesses. Meanwhile, many dollars for the unemployed, the poor, the blind, and the disabled, may be taken away. How can any discussion of these matters be carried out in short, loud bursts on television?

In Geneva, negotiators for the United States and the Soviet Union are meeting to seek some way out of the terrible nuclear confrontation. Our country seems to be sliding into a bog of Central American quicksand. The Congress has on its agenda a sweeping revision of the federal criminal law. These subjects also call for much explanation and public debate.

They will inevitably slow the pace of any news program that takes them up. But they are the stuff of our national life. The people expect us to inform them about these things, and if we don't, who will? If the people are given baby food when they are hungry for a meal of information, they will be undernourished and weakened—and then what will become of the country that is the last, best hope of man?

The best minds in television news are thinking more about packaging and promotion and pace and image and blinking electronics than about thoughtful coverage of the news. I have worked in the field for twenty-five years, and every year I thought we were getting better. Suddenly, I think we're getting worse.

10.

Television's Way with Words

Edwin Newman

I have, while watching television, recently learned the following:

Zest soap, by its own admission, "lathers up pretty good." You can, therefore, wash pretty good with it.

A man who went into the Washington Monument with a gun was "successfully persuaded to come out." Successful persuasion is more effective than unsuccessful persuasion.

Heavyweight fighter Gerry Cooney has been "faithful to his destiny." This was revealed by HBO and must have come as a relief to those who feared that Cooney's devotion to his destiny was flagging and that he thought he could get away from it. While clinging to his destiny, by the way, Cooney fought Larry Holmes in "a twenty-square-foot ring," meaning that it was five feet by four feet, or ten by two, or possibly twenty by one, which would have made for a shorter fight.

The Democrats charged that, thanks to Republican budget plans, "the poor are again being abandoned at the expense of the military." The "CBS Evening News" reported this at the expense of the Democrats, who had charged approximately the opposite.

These are small matters, I suppose, but they are representative of the language on television news and sports programs and in the commercials that pay for them. It is a language often incorrect, often relying on "journalese," and sometimes completely illogical.

The journalese is everywhere: President Reagan made "a major speech" in which "he blasted the Russians." Beirut is the "beleaguered capital" of a "war-torn" or "embattled" or "war-shattered" country. Israel is "the Jewish state," of which Menachem Begin is "the Jewish leader." The United Nations is "the whole body." Oh yes— "awesome," "perception," and "historic." Also "address," "vowed," "officials," and "controversial." Let us say that a perception, awesome in its dimensions, was addressed by officials who vowed something, if possible something historic but at least controversial, leading to a bombshell development that caused a dramatic shakeup. That would be an ideal story, still more so if it began with what "sources said" was a "clash of perceptions," once known as a disagreement.

Here are some other gems, picked up in a short period of random viewing:

General Basilio Lami Dozo, commander of the Argentine Air Force, may be referred to as General Dozo (CNN) and may be reached in the Argentine capital, which is "Bwo-nos Air-ees" (CNN and almost everybody else).

More Spanish: Somebody—I wish I had written down his name—is "an affectionado of baseball."

More English: People in the real estate business are real-a-tors (CBS).

Still more English: If one takes sides in the Middle East, one is either pro-Israel or pro-Arabist (CBS), which means that one favors Israel or favors the specialized study of the Arabic language and culture.

A man called in by ABC News to say that last winter's snow and cold were bad for business was a "weather impact analyst."

"Despite demonstrations by PLO supporters," Menachem Begin made his scheduled speech to the Disarmament Conference of the United Nations. This non sequitur, of a kind one hears over and over again, was supplied by a CBS correspondent who seemed to think that because supporters of the PLO were demonstrating, Begin might not speak.

There are "pro- and anti-nuclear weapons supporters." If they are supporters, the pro isn't needed. If they are anti, they're not supporters.

Sugar Ray Leonard, according to HBO, is "the most popular athlete in the United States of any persuasion." Leonard's religion was not given.

Roberto Duran, facing the aforesaid Leonard of any persuasion, suffered (on HBO) "an ignomonious defeat."

During a fire, flames "bellowed from the upper floors." There was no word on what they told the local correspondent who reported this.

At the beginning of John Hinckley's trial, CBS reported that the outcome "will turn on whether or not he was sane or insane" at the time he shot President Reagan. A remarkable double redundancy, that. In any case, Hinckley undoubtedly was sane or insane at that time. Everybody was.

When President Reagan made known Alexander Haig's resignation as secretary of state, this was a "major announcement."

In an Atari commercial, a young man, faintly astonished, tells a young woman, "You did better than me." Perhaps he should have gone all the way: "You did better than me did."

I have been urged while watching to "Make it a good day," and to "Have a good day," a good evening, a *good* evening, a good night, and a good week, and to enjoy my Saturday morning. Plus I got "Be well" and "Enjoy," with no time limit attached. I wish I could enjoy. The language of television doesn't much help.

One thing more: Could the various anchors stop telling one another the news, as in, "And in the Gulf of Oman, Jim," and tell it to the viewers, instead?

11.

Living in a Nielsen Republic

Les Brown

S
omething that happened at a screening I attended recently made me realize how American values have changed in a scant few years. A group of us attending a communications conference agreed to look at filmed highlights of a public-interest event held in Washington during the final year of the Carter Administration. Everyone dozed for the first few minutes—it was that kind of film—and then Ralph Nader appeared on the screen delivering a speech. Spontaneously, at the sight of him, the audience erupted in laughter. Minutes later Nicholas Johnson, the one-time gadfly of the broadcast industry, came on; again the room went up in howls. Nader and Johnson could have been Olsen & Johnson.

I was puzzled and dismayed. These were not fat cats and tories who were so amused, but academics, technologists, writers, and lawyers—people who, I would guess, once admired Nader and Johnson as courageous social reformers, and probably even supported them. Nobody laughed at these leaders of the activist movements during the seventies, although many cursed them.

But the seventies were gone; so were the styles and rhetoric of the decade. And here on the screen were Nader and Johnson, just as before, fierce, determined, and calling for some kind of justice. What provoked the laughter, of course, was the anachronism: We had changed with the eighties, and they had not. It was like watching old home movies and seeing ourselves dressed in Nehru jackets and flared slacks. There was another comic element—futility. Nothing they were saying was going to matter, not in these times.

In the political atmosphere that brought in Reaganomics, "unregulation," and the shibboleth "no free lunch," the social idealists are absurd throwbacks to a time when our government and national conscience could be stirred by moral arguments.

The laughter in the screening room confirmed the public-interest movement's decline. But it was also a measure of our own loss of idealism, a negation of what we once were as a society.

We used to speak of ourselves as *citizens,* but the word is scarcely used in the eighties. *Citizens* has attained a certain subversive ring. It conjures up people with causes, who interfere with business—people who make public nuisances of themselves, who organize in groups and march on Washington, or challenge the licenses of broadcasters. Citizens always seem to be demanding rights, which in the minds of Washington officials is the same as demanding a free lunch. The private citizen, almost by definition, must somehow be accommodated by government; that does not square with the new view in Washington that the good American fends for himself.

Government prefers to think of us today not as citizens but as *consumers,* the purchasers of products and services. The consumer has the dignity of acting in his own behalf and paying his own way. His demands are not for rights but for conveniences, comforts, material things, and lower prices. What the government can do for him is to deregulate the airline industry, so flights to California can be cheaper. The consumer is the perfection of the citizen, because he doesn't interfere with business. Indeed, the consumer is what business is all about.

These—for pity's sake—are the values of television come to life, the fruits of thirty-five years of commercial bombardment. We have finally become those people in the commercials who live and die by floor waxes and freeze-dried coffee. Television was never really our window on the world, but neither was it our mirror, until now. We have come to see ourselves today as television has always seen us—not as a national community but as components of an economic system. Consumers.

The consumer's habitat is the marketplace, where all great domestic issues are to be resolved. For it is where the consumer asserts his supreme right—the right to buy—and, in doing so, takes part in the continuing referendum we now call "market forces." The marketplace demolishes the idea of government regulation in the public interest; instead it nourishes what some consider a purer form of democracy, one that would have people decide, through the choices they make, what is best for them and their countrymen. Which ultimately means, except to the naive, that business decides.

This new model for American democracy—in which the public interest is defined as what the public is interested in, rather than what is just and healthy for the entire society—has an antecedent. It is, of all things, the television rating system, the viewing referendum that allows broadcasters to boast of television as a cultural democracy.

Through all the years, broadcasters have maintained that people take an active part in television because they speak through the Nielsen ratings. According to this argument, it has always been the public, and not the broadcaster, who decides which programs survive and which get canceled. The broadcaster is ruled by public opinion, as expressed in the Nielsen popularity polls. Congressional committees and the Federal Communications Commission are comfortable with this reasoning. The viewer, exults FCC chairman Mark Fowler, "can vote with the dial." What could be more democratic?

The argument sounds right, but then sophistry always does. In the first place, the people who speak through the Nielsen ratings are not the public but the viewers. The public is all 220 million Americans; the viewers are merely an audience, sometimes immense in size, sometimes only large. But on any given night, more people are not watching prime-time television than are watching the biggest Nielsen hit. More people, for example, reject "Three's Company" than flock to it; yet the sense of the ratings is that the program reflects American mores and tastes. Under the ratings system, the people not watching television don't count; their vote is considered neutral, although implicitly it is negative. All that can truly be claimed for "Three's Company" is that it's a good business because it has struck a lush market. This has to do with consumers, not with citizens.

And not everyone who speaks through the Nielsens really has a voice; only those who matter to advertisers are heard. No broadcaster is especially anxious to reach the elderly and the indigent because they have little discretionary income and aren't sought by advertisers. The best markets for broadcasters are people in the age range of eighteen to forty-nine, since they are the targets for most advertised products. Since buying power is what matters, nearly every program in prime time aims at the same segment, people in the young-adult category.

Despite their numbers in the society, old people, poor people, and young children (except on Saturday mornings), scarcely participate in this viewing referendum. They are equally disenfranchised in the radio marketplace. One of the large Northern talk stations that specializes in telephone call-ins deliberately screens out the callers with creaky voices, because it doesn't want advertisers to think it attracts elderly listeners. Meanwhile, there are some 8,000 commercial radio stations in the United States, and not one of them aims at children twelve and under. Very few devote even as much as an hour a week to this important part of the public. The democracy of market forces is no democracy to those who don't constitute a sufficient market. Yet the FCC is anxious to deregulate radio, satisfied that the public interest will be served by market forces.

Says Mark Fowler, "We have passed the point where reliance on the marketplace is merely a regulatory trend. It has become a social imperative, a commercial imperative, and a constitutional imperative."

And now that we accept ourselves as a nation of consumers, we are prepared to elevate Nielsen democracy to a larger, more consequential political stage. In trusting that consumers will make wiser decisions than the public officials we have elected by ballot, we are actually changing the nature of the vote.

Sparing government the delicate task, the marketplace is deciding for the rest of America which of the new communications technologies should survive, how fast they should grow, and what kinds of programs and services they should offer. This is not the marketplace of ordinary television viewers, but the marketplace of people who can afford to buy the gadgetry. Thus, the poor blacks of the South, who have only recently gained a vote at the polls, have in effect lost part of it already.

Says Mark Fowler: "I have great faith in the future of communications in this country, for I have great faith in . . . the ingenuity of markets to meet the people's needs at the right price."

At the moment, consumer democracy has found that sports, pornography, and made-for-television religion are good for America. Culture is not. Can't sell it.

So we burst into laughter at Ralph Nader and Nick Johnson, as a couple of nuts out of their time and still dead-serious, who tied business into knots in the seventies, who got carried away with themselves as folk heroes, and to whom people in government today have grown deaf. Too bad for us. Whatever their failings, Nader and Johnson don't deserve ridicule, unless we would mock a tradition reaching back through the entire history of our republic, a tradition of public advocates who believe in government for all the people.

Without them and their kind, there is no force to countervail the moneyed interests that put business ahead of social values and that, in the marketplace democracy, stand to win every time. I question that we are merely buyers of products and services; we are not "economic man." The markets that command Mark Fowler's faith do not provide for such values as morals, justice, fairness, and equality. Public interest is not the plural of self-interest.

As a member of the public, as a consumer, citizen, and patriot, I reject the portrayal of our country as a mere marketplace. I reject the idea that I am voting for something when I buy a subway token or have my shoes repaired. Talk about marketplace—is the junkie voting for something when he buys heroin? How seriously do we take *that* vote as an expression of the public interest? There's no denying the interest, or the market forces.

Says Mark Fowler, who has come into our lives through the political patronage system: "A reliance on market forces, not on dubious value judgments of insulated regulators, is the next right step." And: "From here onward, the public's interest must determine the public interest."

Pass the heroin.

12.

Escapist Realism

Brian Winston

Norman Lear, Captain of the Adult Army in the service of the Republic of Realism, has won in recent years many famous victories over the Kingdom of Bland. There were the skirmishes at Fornication and Blasphemy, the repeated assaults to establish a bridgehead in Adultery, the struggle on the Heights of Masturbation, the battle at the Pass of Menopause, the campaign on the Plains of Homosexuality and, above all, the debacle in Ethnic Minorities. Bland has had but one success, off the Gulf of Violence; she has groaned for several years under the heel of Realism.

Yet the war is thought to be still unresolved, and within the Kingdom of Bland (which some name Righteous) a secret leader has arisen, called Falwell. It has been said that he has a weapon, a bomb called "Majority," with which he will scatter all the forces of Realism.

This promised counterattack, coming as it has on the crest of other moves to the Right, has alarmed many. But the argument is not as black and white as either side would have us believe.

Unless we share the fundamentalist faith, which seems to see television as the work of the Devil, we are unlikely to support any "clean up television" campaigns. We will be more concerned with freedom of speech. But is the notion that television ought to respect the sensibilities of its audience, a notion underlying at least part of the New Right's rhetoric, so unacceptable in a democracy? Conversely, is the argument so self-evident that any diminution of the industry's freedoms must lead inevitably to other curtailments? It is repeated often enough to assume the force of law—but is there no distinction to be drawn between the magnified discourse of those privileged few who use the media, and the speech of the rest of us?

This debate of principles rages so furiously that we seldom seem to get down to the nitty-gritty of the programs themselves. In fact, for the Liberal/Realist side, *discussion* about the content of the programs seems nothing so much as an early threat to First Amendment rights.

Lear is prepared to talk about content, though. He sees the new openness as a series of victories. Sexual explicitness becomes some sort of yardstick—a measure by which a television service shall be judged mature, relevant, and of public value. I think he does himself a profound disservice by arguing in this way. He is a producer whose concerns and whose programs are greater than this. But the climate for which he has struggled does not tend in general to inspire work as good as his.

"Three's Company," for example, is a successful situation comedy in the modern manner. Based on a British model, it concerns a man and two women sharing an apartment. The situation is funny because the laws of the world in which it is set are as follows: 1) Homosexuals do not fornicate with women; 2) fornication must be prevented; 3) no heterosexual man can share living space with a woman without fornicating with her; ergo, 4) the man must not share with the women because he will fornicate with them, unless 5) he is a homosexual. Thus, in order to keep his room, the hero of the series pretends to be gay. The landlord is placated by this ruse—which amuses because he ought stereotypically to be more appalled by any thought of homosexuality than by heterosexual fornication, but is not. The hero, although he is a womanizer, does not fornicate with the women. One of the women has big mammaries. (This pornographic world has an implied subrule to rule 3 above, which reads, "Men's lust is in direct proportion to the size of women's mammaries.")

The Reverend Jerry Falwell, I assume, finds "Three's Company" deeply offensive. And (I assume for different reasons) so do I. It is, among other things, the most consistently homophobic show on television—although "Sheriff Lobo" tried hard for this title and on occasion so, too, do almost all of the other sitcoms. I have trouble with the Liberal/Realist position on this because I am by no means convinced that we as a society are ready for a steady stream of homophobic jokes. If I am asked whether homophobic jokes are better than no mention of homosexuality at all, I am afraid I must take a raincheck.

Once upon a time, before Lucille Ball got pregnant, American television eschewed all references to human sexuality. Most thinking people considered this at best strange, and at worst very bad. The assumption made by both parties to this debate, Right and Realist, is that television is part of society. Realists (and myself) make a further assumption that it ought to reflect society. For intelligent and concerned professionals, the dominance of blandness was inhibiting, silly, and finally degrading. So the battle for relaxation of sexual mores that was taking place in society at large was joined by many in, and on, television.

In television as in society, it was not just sex that was at stake, but also race. In the time before Lucy was expelled from the Garden, the only blacks we saw were "Amos 'n' Andy." Instead of a black reality at a time of extremely important change, we had black stereotyping—bland black stereotyping.

The battle was waged to open television on a number of fronts so that a more accurate picture of society could be reflected. But between the successful undertaking of this quite proper campaign for a more adult agenda and "Three's Company" (or "Too Close for Comfort," or "documentaries" about every form of sexual deviancy, or a host of other shows), something seems to have gone terribly wrong.

The depiction of sex is not, of and in itself, mature and relevant. In fact, of and in itself it is more likely to be juvenile and scatological. We have had long periods wherein no frank representations of sex were allowed, and in equally long periods (in alternating fashion) we have had greater explicitness. The pendulum's swing seems to have little to do with the general state of society, whatever moralists may claim about the Fall of Rome and the like. (England's first empire was founded in a period of comparative sexual laxity and her second in a period of restraint, for instance.) But more important than this, restraint or permissiveness has nothing to do with the maturity or relevance of art works. Books, plays, and films that speak eloquently to the human condition in general and to relations between the sexes in particular have been produced without explicit material; just as permissiveness has produced stilted, sexually graphic, jejune garbage. So the analysis was right—bland is bad for both television and society; but the solution—sex is everything and jokes about it are liberating—was wrong.

Take jokes: In a society where many deem deep inequalities (as between the races, or between men and women, or because of sexual preference) to exist, it is not emancipating to make these various elements the butt of humor and leave it there. There is a profound difference between laughing at those in authority and laughing at those without power. The one leads to *A Modest Proposal* and the best tradition of open, healthy criticism; the other leads to those films the Nazis shot in concentration camps for their own amusement.

It is no good claiming that laughter is automatically healthy. The Elizabethans thought insanity hilarious and had no inhibitions about dealing with it in literature and on the stage. Much good that did for the insane!

So although blacks have come a long way from "Amos 'n' Andy," my worry is that they have come further on the screen than they have in the street. A similar gap exists for homosexuals, women, and others. And that gap between the real situation and the picture created by "realistic" television is as dangerous as the old gap between escapism and the world beyond. It is as if the television industry has enlarged the poorly silvered mirror it once held up to society to include more, with the silvering remaining as patchy and distorting as ever.

Jane Austen is not likely to titillate anybody. Compared with our output of programs she is repressed indeed. Yet it is perhaps instructive to note, as a measure of how far or how little we have progressed towards the adult, that one of her major subjects is curiously lacking from our emancipated fare. The subject is money. For Austen, people's standing in society, what living they have, is crucially important. For us, that "Laverne & Shirley" were working girls was evidenced in the original series by still photographs flashed up for seconds in the title sequence. Even in those shows with work as their setting, it counts for very little. Loni Anderson, the sensitive unstereotyped blonde in "WKRP in Cincinnati," walked away from a job as a radio personality and back to her reception desk without the money involved ever being hinted at—just as Victorians might never talk of sex.

But more is at stake here than simply swapping one forbidden area for another. The whole case for greater sexual realism rests on a belief that it is important for television to look unblinking at the whole world of which it is a part. We live in a violent, problem-ridden, and sometimes ugly society that we need to confront and deal with; television, realistic television, is supposed to help us do that. Instead, we have television that will sell us sanitary napkins but that cannot make jokes about wages.

As far as money and class are concerned, television is as much of a dreamworld as ever it was in the fifties; more, perhaps, because where is "Life of Riley"? As far as women are concerned, there are still very few positive role-models—one female (in "Bosom Buddies") is a boss, but she presides over two guys who, for the sake of living accommodation again, spend half their time in drag. What kind of world is that?

Quite often the victory of realism means talking out of both sides of the mouth at once. "The Facts of Life" is a situation comedy set with breathtaking social blindness in the privileged world of boarding schools. Here, the nascent sexuality of the young females is a prime source of humor; but occasionally, as in an episode that had the youngest child becoming a model, the audience can be given an appropriate lesson in the immorality of all such exploitation.

I know of no finer exemplum of racial harmony than the one existing in the strange household of Mr. Drummond of Park Avenue (the good part), New York City, with his (obligatory?) lack of wife and his three children—two black, one white—and his absolutely startling lack of financial cares. This is a world of "Diff'rent Strokes" indeed. Gary Coleman, the small black child with the perfect comedy timing, is more than occasionally the excuse for moralizing. (The laugh track tends to go "ah" and "ooh" at such moments.) But I have never seen a racist appear on this show—that is, somebody who believes "some races are by nature superior to others," specifically the white race to the black. Arnold, Coleman's character, is always encountering "bigots," that is, "one intolerantly devoted to his own church, party, or opinion," and not the same thing as a racist in this man's dictionary.

I must not give the impression that the realist effort has been entirely confined to such glories as a local news program's searing series of exposés of incest during a sweep week. There is "M*A*S*H" (which, Atlas-like, must bear the whole output on its admittedly broad back), "Barney Miller," and "Taxi" —comedies that bring a new air of manners to television. I look at "Lou

Grant", which attempts, however melodramatically and super-ficially, to enlarge our understanding of the world. I have enjoyed serious dramas on serious themes—a few; but overwhelmingly, these have been too many prurient and titillating exercises on the lives of teenage hitchhikers, escorts, lustful female teachers, and the like. Sex still means mainly sniggers, giggles, and smirks; there are still no "racists"; there is still very little "work."

Now comes Mr. Falwell, who would abridge the essential right to reflect the world and apparently much else besides. What in truth can we say to him and those whom he leads? It seems to me the Adult Army has nearly sold the pass, and that a great cause has been tarnished and trivialized by a tide of escapist, salacious, mealy-mouthed, second-rate programs. In reality, it is no good to say freedom must mean freedom to be silly and slightly disgust-ing. In reality, freedom of speech needs to be exercised with a greater sense of how mighty a privilege it really is.

Of course I will go to the gallows defending the right of the makers of "Three's Company" to produce whatever garbage they want—but I will go kicking and screaming. The mob, with more reason than usual, is dangerously close to having all our heads.

13.

The "Video Revolution" and Human Nature

William A. Henry III

You come home from a hard day at the office. You shrug off your jacket, kick off your shoes, wonder aloud about dinner, and start planning how to unwind for the evening. You could sit down with a small-print catalogue of 3,000 video cassettes available for sale at the local dealers. You could comparison-shop between that catalogue and the listing for 1,800 video discs. You could turn on the television to the directory channel and try to choose an evening's viewing from among the other 119 channels. Or you could study the printed viewer guide if all the flickering white type on the directory channel made your eyes hurt.

After you narrowed your choice down to the seven or so programs you wanted to watch sooner or later, all of them running on recycling loops throughout the month, you could program the home computer with your work and social schedules and have it tell you which show you could watch now without losing the chance to see the others later. Until your selection started you could play a video game or tap into the news headlines (it would require only nine typed responses) from the video-data stream fed by telephone wires into your set.

Or you could give the whole thing up as more work than it's worth, go upstairs to bed, and open a book.

The foregoing scenario of the "home entertainment center"

after the "video revolution" has been presented by stockmarket visionaries, company salesmen, and gadget freaks as the ultimate liberation of the mass mind. I suspect that instead, it may be a massive boondoggle based on a gross misunderstanding of human nature.

People like a limited field of choice. Ask a child which of two things he'd like to do and he will answer promptly. Ask him which of seven and he will fall silent. Ask an adult in a restaurant which of ten desserts he'd like and he'll tell you to come back in a few minutes. Take him for the first time to a Chinese restaurant with a six-page menu and he'll mutter all night.

It's always hard to sort out cause and effect. But I guess we may have developed three networks (four including PBS) not only because of economic and technological limitations, but also because that is about the maximum number of options most people want to consider. The public's taste seems to be maturing, and in the process fragmenting, as people define more precisely what they want to watch. But if three or four copycat networks are not enough, if people grouse (and not all that often) that there's nothing they want to watch on four channels, it does not necessarily follow that they are asking for, say, eight dozen.

To some extent, visions of the future are known to be pipe dreams anyway. There is not, and there probably will not be, enough unduplicated programming to fill all those channels, nor the economics to justify them, nor the audience to view them. Even the most hooked can watch only so many hours of television a day. And the most hooked often aren't watching, strictly speaking. They are using the set as companion or background noise. Almost any mass-appeal channel will serve the purpose. The hooked can't be bothered to turn the dial every half-hour, Nielsen and network researchers tell us. They surely won't be poring over catalogues to figure out what to see (or rather hear) next in their twelve-hour television day.

Our society already suffers from an information glut. Print and especially television news flood us with unassimilated facts. Advertising wizards, who are usually ahead of the rest in the word-business, recognized that reality a while ago and started to emphasize feelings rather than statistics. How will the hassled, over-informed public react when asked to study and memorize a viewing schedule, each hour of which is more complicated than an anatomy chart?

There are subtler questions, too. How much of the public's

pleasure in watching television is tied to the fact that almost everyone else is watching the same things at the same time—and thus can find a natural topic of conversation at the office, supermarket, or laundromat the next day? From my observation, television has surpassed the weather as the great unifying subject of American chitchat. The video revolution would diminish, if not eliminate, that unity.

The revolution would also diminish, if not wreck, the star system. What would we do for heroes, sex objects, surrogate friends, if we did not share nationally recognizable performers or roles? Less lavish productions made for smaller audiences might or might not fulfill our individual needs for fantasy as effectively. But it may be important to our fantasies to know they are shared by others, that we are worshipping at a popular altar.

The video revolution would also have profoundly disruptive effects on major American institutions—advertisers and their corporate clients, politics and government—which would likely fight anything obstructing their ease of access to the common people.

But they may not have to fight after all. I suspect most of the public likes television reasonably well as it is. There is bound to be an upscale market for discs and cassettes (though thus far it is for porno and movies, the latter a limited product and the former reaching a limited audience). There is evident enthusiasm in places like Columbus, Ohio, for the add-on services cable can offer. Yet despite Warner Communications' massive investment there (they don't call it losses, they call it research and development), cable channels outdraw the networks only with major movies, prime local sports events, and two or three televised town meetings per year. Jimmied and unreliable as the Nielsen numbers may be, they reflect a reality we all can affirm. A great many people watch a lot of network television and most get a lot of pleasure from it, or at least enough pleasure not to pursue anything more active. They don't read books or take courses in Chinese. Why, then, will they want television to change so that they have to read a viewer guide as thick as a book, or program a computer in a language as alien as Chinese? They might as likely throw out the dog and the slippers.

14.

Living with a Satellite Dish

Steven Levy

The Barlow home looks like any other rambling house in rural Connecticut: considerably more than a hundred years old, but well-kept, with a recent coat of white paint. The family is right on the demographic money—Portus Barlow, a thirty-one-year-old executive, wife Kathy, nine-year-old Shanthi, and six-year-old Silas. But my reason for visiting them one recent weekend stands behind their house: a twelve-foot square apparatus made by Barlow's company, which manufactures satellite receiving dishes. Made of screening and redwood scaffolding, it looks like a giant hibachi. It's called a Skyview 1 earth station antenna; it enables any home to pull in transmissions bounced off space satellites: thousands of choices that allegedly transform an ordinary television into the world's most varied programming source.

I had heard the wondrous stories about the visual options available to those few who had taken the expensive plunge and installed a "dish" beside their hot tub or tennis court. They have free access to dozens of pay-television services, enough sports events to make every day an Olympian orgy, and even some literal orgies to satisfy the most prurient of videophiles. Also, they get voyeuristic looks at network "feeds" not intended for broadcast: disparaging remarks muttered by newspersons beaming their reports to home bases in New York or Atlanta; behind-the-scenes caucuses of sports announcers between innings, and the much-touted antics of Johnny Carson during station breaks. I imagined Johnny uncensored, uttering pithy, unprintable remarks that convulse the studio audience (as well as the fortunate dish owners watching the NBC satellite feed to affililates).

On the other hand, I had my doubts about the joys of dish owning. Earth station reception is a true do-it-yourself alternative to conventional television reception, and I wasn't sure how well it worked, technically or aesthetically. Then there was the cost. Could *anything* justify the price tag of $3,000 to $10,000 for a home setup?

Some of my qualms vanished within minutes of arriving at my earth station destination, bucolic Putnam, Connecticut. I headed straight for the family's nineteen-inch color television. Since Portus Barlow is in the dish business, he was only too happy to flick on the set. After spinning the knobs of the in-home receiver, which is the size of a fat cigar box, we got an image. It looked like any other sharp television image. In fact, I recognized it: the relentlessly cute mug of little Tracy, heroine of *Oh God! Book II.* I had caught a half-hour of this pious calamity the week before, hoping for distraction from work, but I could not deal with mediocrity on such a cosmic plane, and had returned to my typewriter a beaten man. Now, with a helping hand from outer space, I was once again suffering that child's conversations with deity George Burns.

Barlow informed me that I was receiving this signal from Transponder 12 on the Satcom satellite. What this meant, I learned, was that the dish in the backyard could bring in up to eleven satellites, but the horn-like amplifier poised a few feet away from the dish was focused on one in particular: RCA's Satcom IIIR. On that satellite, or "bird," are twenty-four transponders bouncing back signals sent from earth. Each transponder has its own frequency, and I could switch to another transponder—change the channel—by turning a knob on the receiver beside me. Which I promptly did.

The goodies of Satcom IIIR revealed themselves to me—an all-star squad of cable-network services. Barlow told me Satcom's lineup was so impressive that he almost never adjusted his equipment to pull in the other satellites. I could see why. A quick switch of the dial yielded Nicholson and Dunaway emoting away in *Chinatown* (The Movie Channel); an ESPN quarterback reading the Ottawa blitz; Todd Rundgren going through visual changes on Music Television (MTV); a CNN report on New York singles; a Christian talk show for kids, interrupted by a message to would-be suicides; a Cinemax French film about a lady cop, with fleeting nudity; and more movies, two commercial-free cartoon shows . . . a virtual cornucopia. All in an area that barely receives the signals of the three major network affiliates in Boston, and has no cable hookup or subscription television.

"I can't remember the last time I watched broadcast television," says Portus Barlow. He confided that, really, he's too busy to watch much television at all. Kathy Barlow told me the same thing, and added that she tries to keep the kids' watching to a minimum. But as the weekend progressed, I found that satellite viewing had perhaps more of an effect on the Barlows than they admitted. As almost every movie came on, or was previewed—and there were scores of them—Portus or Kathy would provide an informed critique. (And the opinion hadn't been formed in a theater—Barlow says he hasn't been out to the movies in years, since they're all on his screen within months of release.)

What the parents had not seen, the kids had. During a Showtime presentation of the *The Idolmaker,* the teen idol at one point talked a naïve fan into a compromising position in his car. "She's only fourteen!" six-year-old Silas shouted with glee, much as a pre-space-age child would have shouted, "Watch out for the witch!" to Hansel and Gretel. Silas and his brother were also uncannily familiar with the groups whose promotional clips are shown as the programming mainstay of MTV on Transponder 11. Before a chord is played, Silas will identify the band, be they the Pretenders or some obscure heavy-metal contingent, and voice his opinion on the upcoming visual effects. The opinion is usually favorable; MTV gives kids the same kind of short-term gratification as "Sesame Street," though it does so somewhat more loudly.

Mostly what the Barlows watch, though, and what I watched while snatching signals from Satcom IIIR, are movies. With the giants of pay television coming in free, this is not surprising. It is also a less varied menu than one might suspect; the repetition can be numbing. For example, by using different transponders, I could watch my old nemesis *Oh God! Book II* not once, but *eight* times in a little over the first twenty-four hours of my visit. And the aforementioned *Idolmaker* was shown almost as many times. This is not my idea of a brave new world. The system is fine as long as you haven't seen the film yet and need plenty of chances to catch it from the beginning. But after seeing a movie, a dish owner may run across it again literally hundreds of times. This makes the rerun policy of the three broadcast networks seem rather benign

Fortunately, there are always twenty or so other choices to make on Satcom IIIR. And having *all* the movie channels means you won't miss out on some of the modest yet compelling films shown on only one or two services. You get into the habit of changing the channel rather often, rolling dice for something better than what's presently on. Sometimes you roll lucky seven—a viewing of *Bananas* on Home Theater Network, or Fernando Valenzuela pitching against the Cubs on WGN. Other times, the dice come up snake eyes, and you get George Burns in his Jehovah mode.

To get this kind of variety on cable (and no cable company offers this kind of variety), you'd have to pay steep monthly fees. After shelling out the initial cost, though, earth station owners pay zilch for "premium" services. Even if they *want* to pay, programmers such as HBO and Showtime refuse to accept their money. Pay-television executives have a term for the practice of watching their offerings by dish: theft of signal.

They say they will eventually scramble their transmissions so only cable operators with decoders will be able to use them. "If people buy earth stations thinking they're in for all this free entertainment, they're going to have a shock—before long, even the nonpremium services will scramble," says a Showtime executive. But cynics point out that the number of earth station owners seems too small to justify the cost of developing a fool-proof scrambler and equipping thousands of cable operators with decoders.

The present, of course, is still blissfully unscrambled. And I was getting quite comfortable with Satcom IIIR. But its riches of sports, movies, and polyester preachers were not enough—almost a dozen other "birds" were waiting to be plucked. On these, I hoped to see some of the exotica that dish watching is noted for. But unless your dish is equipped with an expensive motorized switching mechanism (few dishes are), you have to go outside and repoint the dish or its amplifier until it's aimed directly at the satellite you want. As someone who frequently balks at getting off the sofa to change channels, I find the idea of going outside on a winter's night to switch satellites rather hellish. But it was spring, so Barlow and I went across town to his office, behind which was a dish set up for serious satellite hunting, or "cherry picking."

Portus Barlow and I spent Saturday night trying to find orbiting birds. After cranking the dish toward what we thought was a satellite and coming up blank a few times, we finally picked one up and went inside to watch it. Only three transponders were active: some Christian network, an auxiliary Cinemax channel, and the prize, R-rated Escapade, which at the moment was showing some foreign, grade-Z titillation flick with a dubbing job that must have been done by actors on Quaaludes. Not that I was listening.

On Sunday afternoon we tried again, with much more success. Barlow had figured out that the previous night's difficulty was due to "reversed polarity," whatever that means. So he reversed our polarity, and things were fine. Using a chart with each satellite's elevation and position on the horizon, we decided which bird we wanted and pointed the dish directly towards its coordinates. Sure enough, we hit the bird each time, and were rewarded with a whole new set of transmissions. This was a rather startling experience for me. I had never doubted the *existence* of these satellites, mind you. It's just that I never expected them to respond to me so personally.

Unfortunately, it was the wrong time for Johnny Carson. But on one of the three Canadian birds we pulled in, we did get a Montreal Expos game with commentary in French. Other Canadian offerings included a show on Chinese cooking (the host wore an apron saying "Eat at Your Own Risk," which I hope does not typify North-of-the-Border humor), a rerun of the television series "Flipper," a religious show from Vancouver, a flick with modern-day cavemen engaged in terrorist activities, a variety show with a slick French crooner, and a highbrow talk show about classical music. On Satcom IV, we got the NBC feed of the Arlington Million horse race, where a flustered announcer (NBC had just identified the wrong winner in a photo finish) asked his director to repeat two simple instructions slowly, then complained, "I need to write that on a card—it's too complicated." Meanwhile, the video portion of this station-break circus showed the race being run at lightning speed—in reverse.

On one of the Westar birds, there were sports: the Red Sox against the A's on the Armed Services Network, the ABC feed of the Redskins exhibition game, and a Los Angeles station's feed of the Angel-Oriole game. While waiting for the broadcast to start, announcer Ron Fairly said to his boothmate Don Drysdale: "What are you going to talk about, big boy?"

Did you ever wonder what cameramen focus on between innings of a ball game? Between frames of the Atlanta game sent to WTBS from Montreal, the video showed a tight, *tight* close-up of a foxy woman returning to her seat in the stands. Her progress was faithfully recorded for the entire trip down the aisle.

Meanwhile, another bird was transmitting four PBS broadcasts to various affiliates. On one, a neatly coiffed interviewer was conducting a dialogue with someone in a distant studio—but this particular feed showed only our interviewer, nodding sagely in response to a voice that only he heard.

Enjoyable as they are, these "inside" feeds are novelties that I suspect dish owners soon tire of. After a few hours of intense satellite and transponder hopping, I was ready to chuck it all and watch just *one* close baseball game, or just *one* good movie. In two days of almost nonstop viewing, I had seen, aside from a few quirky things, nothing truly memorable—just much more of some of the better or worse things I usually saw. Portus Barlow summed it up when he told me, "No matter how good a delivery system is, it can't make up for a lack of software."

So my conclusion was that for folks living in some obscure corner of Idaho—or any area without cable or subscription television—dish owning might well be salvation, at least until the scramblers come. But for a conventionally wired New Yorker, satellite television is a high-priced smorgasbord. A few rare spices have been added, but the food is essentially the same as what you get at home—only in much larger quantities. I left stuffed, and was glad I came . . . but after all, I didn't have to foot the bill.

15.

What Harm to the Children?

Robert Coles

When I was in medical school I very much wanted to be a pediatrician. I took all the electives in that specialty I could manage. Later, I went on to take residency training in the subject before moving in the direction of child psychiatry. A wonderful mentor and friend at the time (the 1950s) was William Carlos Williams, a writing doctor if ever there was one: poet, novelist, playwright, essayist, and not least, a marvelously astute, conscientious "general practitioner," as we used to call an almost forgotten species of physician. At the time "Doc Williams," as he was called, made his home visits among the poor and working-class people of northern New Jersey, Paterson especially. He was attentive to a population some other doctors have chosen to ignore—humble, moneyless, uneducated families—from whom, he kept insisting, he learned a whole lot. The children of those tenement houses particularly impressed him with their vitality, resourcefulness, canniness, their marvelous sense of humor, and, very important, the lessons they kept giving him. No talk about "cultural disadvantage," "cultural deprivation" from him. No inclination on his part to emphasize the flaws, warts, deficits of the "tough kids" (he often called them) who said "hi" and "hi" and "hi" to him as he made his way on daily rounds. Later, well into the evening, he'd pull scraps of paper out of his jacket pockets—words, phrases, entire sentences that had caught his fancy. They became the stuff of his lyrics, his poignant stories, a number of them (those collected as *Life Along the Passaic)* drawn from his medical work with children.

I mention Dr. Williams because I accompanied him, from time to time, as he did his pediatric work, and I talked with him, over a quarter of a century ago, about this country's young—how they contrasted, to his shrewd and knowing eyes, with the boys or girls of an earlier America. He was rather wry, even skeptical, as he heard my excited talk of this and that, the "new influences" I was sure would make life so different for everyone. In a letter once, he was tactful in bringing me up short after hearing me out: "You may be right. Certainly things change over the years. But I often wonder whether the changes are as big and significant as we make them out to be. Don't you think that each generation wants to make *its* mark on history, on the world? Maybe one way to do so is to say: Hey, look at what's happening to *us,* that makes *our* life so very special. I guess I favor waiting and seeing—and keeping an eye on the past, because my hunch is that there's a *sameness* to this life for all of us, the result of what we are: a creature with a certain kind of head and a heart, a limited number of years—what those existentialists talk about."

As for television, increasingly around in the last years of his life (he died in 1963), Williams had no great expectation that it would strongly affect children—a major conviction of mine back then, and one I discussed with him occasionally. I was in my twenties, and I was stunned at the "gap" between my childhood (with the radio and its demands on the listener) and the kind of childhood I was observing as I trained to work with the young—with television and its quite different offerings to a boy or girl viewer. One day I told him that I believed the upcoming generation would be "markedly different," because it would be strongly influenced by the constant visual experiences in the home. He agreed that soon enough television would be virtually every American child's inheritance, of sorts, but he picked me up on the adjective "markedly." He said he remembered the arrival of radio and the movies and he had been sure that children would never quite be the same—all that auditory and visual "input." But he had noticed no real break, on the part of the children he knew, with the essential character of their humanity. They were, still, trying to grow up the best way they knew how, given the ups and downs of their particular family life. They knew, as did children before them, all the big and small emotions: love for parents and warm feelings toward friends and admiration for certain older persons and envy and spite and meanness.

"Whatever they see and hear will have to find a place in a child's life," Williams pointed out, and then he added, "Think of the kids crossing this country in covered wagons; think of the long days across the prairie; think of the coyotes and the buffalo; think of the talk of the Indians, the talk of gold, the talk of the Pacific, and the sight of the Indians and the sight of the desert or the mountains or the canyons or the mighty rivers and finally, the ocean. What 'effect' did all that have on children? They never asked that, our ancestors. We do. The question may be more important than any answer there is to it—and I don't think it's the kind of question that gets one answer. Maybe as many answers as there are children!"

A kind of widsom, that; and a kind I fear I was not very interested in receiving at the time. I was concentrating hard on the likely negative influence of a new aspect of twentieth-century technology; he was reminding me that my overall view of human vulnerability was as significant as my concern about a particular, potentially noxious element of today's world. Like a good social historian, Williams was reminding me that through the generations, children have had to deal with an astonishing array of enticements and hazards. By now, indeed, many of us have absorbed Phillippe Aries's reminder (in *Centuries of Childhood*) that even our notion of when adulthood begins has been, and continues to be, an entirely relative matter—a matter of which culture or people, dealing with what traditions, social obligations, economic limitations, or possibilities. In the nations of the West, until the seventeenth century, an eight- or nine-year-old person was already "grown up" —at work, and regarded as quite responsible, morally, civilly. Put differently, childhood is no exclusive mandate of nature's, but rather has to do with the way we view certain other mandates. For the upper classes of such increasingly industrial, secular countries as France, England, and America, children become an ultimate concern, an abiding preoccupation, a prized possession, to be protected at all costs—the only credible approximation of eternity. In earlier times, of course, children were one's co-workers—there on the farm or in the town's workshop, sweating it out with everyone else. A child old enough, as we see it, to go to school, was a person old enough, as others saw it, to work—and dress like adults, behave like adults, be held morally accountable as adults are.

Through a strange turn of events, we may well be edging back to that earlier notion of childhood. Children of well-to-do families are hardly protected from the onslaughts of the adult world. They are increasingly becoming as worldly, as savvy, as independent as are their grown-up fellow citizens. More and more we learn about the drinking and drug problems of younger and younger children—down to the upper precincts of the elementary-school population. Teenage sexuality and the resulting pregnancies are a severe national problem; and unfortunately, younger adolescents are very much active in that regard. Just as sad is the exploitation of our children by advertisers—for example, the sexual precocity of various girls used cleverly to hustle potential purchasers of one sort or another. In one of the interviews I recently did with a group of suburban school teachers, I heard this from a woman of forty who has been teaching sixth grade in a middle-class New England town for fifteen years: "I can't even remember the 'old days' anymore. Now my pupils are so *worldly.* They know their rock music. They respond not only to the rhythms, but the words, innuendos, and suggestions. They act macho if they are boys, or seductive if they are girls. They've more than tasted beer, or even hard liquor—at least a significant number have. They've looked at *Playboy.* They are very clothes-conscious, and what they wear is meant to show how 'with it' they are. They are thirsting to be 'teenagers' —meaning all taken up with cliques and sexual talk, if not action. I have to pinch myself sometimes and ask, how did all this happen?"

She had much more to say—an astute observer of a swiftly changing American social reality. When I asked her for *her* explanation, I received a demurrer: "I pass! I've blamed everything—affluence, permissiveness, the decline of religion in the lives of people (I mean, as opposed to the showy ritual of going to church!), the rootlessness of families, the increasingly long absence from home of both parents and, of course, television. There was a time when I blamed television more than anything else; I felt these kids I teach are 'tube dazed,' the phrase my husband used. But we've both begun to realize that the tube is just part of a larger story—what's happening to the American family. When I listen to children these days, I hear more than television programs and ads influencing their heads."

At the time, I wasn't so sure she was right to dismiss so readily the impact of television on children. I had in mind a number of studies, which tell us that children who watch some of the violence-filled programs afterwards become excited if not prone to their own kind of truculence. Of course, these are the results of psychological *experiments*—and do not by any means prove that what happens in someone's research situation is what happens in everyday life. No matter, I had in mind my own annoyance, if not disgust, at the programs my children and their friends want to watch—and watch and watch, if not stopped by worrying adults. Is it not a matter of pure common sense that a child who sees meanness and nastiness made a matter of casual, everyday life, is a child put in serious psychological jeopardy? Can it possibly be good, in an ordinary sense of the word "good," that so many of our young sit and watch the silly drivel, the brutish junk that all too many television stations over the country offer, in the morning and in the afternoon, and Lord knows, on Saturday without interruption?

I shared some of those concerns with that teacher, and she nodded in assent at first. But she hastened to offer some thoughtful reservations, which I've not wanted to forget: "You've got to ask yourself *why* —why these kids sit and stare at those shows. I've tried something: I've watched them with some kids, and then I've asked them afterwards what went on, and a lot of the time, they don't remember too well! They will try hard to dredge up something, but usually they speak in generalities: 'It's about this bad guy, and he fools everyone for a long time, but he gets caught in the end.' Or, 'It's about these people out in space, and they are lost, and there are these bad people, and they try to hurt everyone, and they do, but in the nick of time the good people escape.' I'm interested that the children are long on schematic generalizations, I suppose I call them; but short, very short on specifics. I watch them when the specifics are right before them, showing on the television screen, and there seems to be no fear or anguish in the children, but sometimes a laugh or two. I wonder why?

"Actually, I think I know why. The kids aren't looking at the tube the same way I am. What do I mean by that? I mean that these kids are sitting there and listening and looking, but they're not really paying attention. I am! I'm seeing all the ridiculous or awful situations and I'm angry or appalled. The kids are in a bit of a daze—but not because they've been sedated or because they're mesmerized by fear or anxiety. Often I think they are bored silly. They are bored silly in school sometimes, so I know the syndrome. They don't really take in what is being said, even though they seem to be sitting there, looking right at you, and not distracted by anyone or anything. An older teacher I've known for years—she's taught me *so* much!—used to say to me, 'There's a big difference between being there, and putting your mind to work.' I find myself, a lot of the time, practically shouting at the children to *pay attention,* but they're not paying enough attention to begin paying attention, real attention—the kind that means something will stick, sink in, and stay in."

She was quick to apologize for her mere anecdotal and impressionistic vein—her possibly presumptuous subjectivity. But she works with children all the time, is herself a mother—and may well have something to teach us. It is one thing for us to bear down on a given phenomenon, relentlessly analyze it, even make it the subject of research in what is called, these days, social psychology—and quite another matter to figure out how lives get lived, in this case meaning how certain events get worked into the texture of the mind's perceptual and moral life. As a matter of fact, I remember the words of the college professor who supervised the research I did on William Carlos Williams's life and poetry: "I teach these writers, and I wonder how much of what they say, never mind what I say, sticks with my students any longer than five minutes after they've taken the final examination." A moment of despair, maybe. But also, quite possibly, a comment on the way our minds work, no matter our age. We are showered all the time by stimuli—the continual press of sights and sounds upon the limited terrain of our awareness. We work harder than we know, as Freud repeatedly reminded us, to push things aside, tuck them away, consign them to the spacious oblivion we call, in our time, the unconscious. This forgetfulness is not by any means all bad. It can be a great and necessary friend. Plenty of the mind's troubles, the world's drab or sinister reality, get screened from our notice.

In my experience with various kinds of American adults and children, television programs have a short mental life, so far as the viewer goes—often for sad reasons, indeed: "I watch a lot, and so I can't always recall what I saw. I get mixed up. I confuse one program with another sometimes. There will be times I watch just enough to pretend I've seen the program so I can keep up with my friends when they talk about it." Not an elderly, slightly disoriented person, fighting hard against the ravages of senility, but a ten-year-old boy willing to be candid about his viewing time, the nature of his friendships. How much, many of us wonder, can anyone possibly absorb—from the endless parade of visual banality? Rather a lot, I fear. Absorb, and often enough forget or bury. Several times that same child told me he fell asleep watching a series of Saturday morning cartoons. He himself was shrewd enough to remind me that there was no good physiological reason for that to have happened: "I went to bed early, and slept all night. I wasn't tired when I woke up." I decided to press a point home: Was he, maybe, a bit bored? No, he insisted, his eyes now open wider than usual. He was alert to yet another adult's around-the-corner preachiness. His own parents were often quick to deny him television—yet he watched it and watched it. All too commonly, they were not home, in fact, to stop him.

I have no wish to defend our networks from the oft-stated charges of misfeasance, malfeasance, and nonfeasance with respect to their responsibilities toward our younger television-viewing population. Trash is produced in abundance; trash is seen and seen; trash cannot but remind our boys and girls, once more, how terribly cynical and disappointing certain aspects of this life turn out to be. Trash can also, surely, give a sanctioning, external nod to the trashier side of one or another child's psychological life. I have known troubled children who pick up cues from radio programs, from the lyrics of rock music, from television, and yes, from reading matter: comic books, so-called adventure stories, spy thrillers, even what many of us adults would deem to be "good fiction." For example, what is so reassuring, sound, and instructive about Maurice Sendak's pictures and stories? Some of us adults find him a first-rate artist and storyteller—imaginative and uniquely talented. We are told that children, as well, love his work. No doubt many do—or pick up the attitude of their elders, and respond similarly. Some don't, however. I know children who find Sendak's stories "strange," or "no good," and who find his drawings "scary" or "nuts" or "real, real strange." I know other children, especially those already struggling with the quite real fearfulness of ghetto life, who find Sendak, and others in the tradition of romantically extravagant and humorous storytelling for children, impossibly cute, coy, unappealing—even maddening. "Who in hell is supposed to read all that loony stuff? Kids who have nothing to do but sit and make up stranger and stranger things in their heads, and think how smart they are for doing it. If they come here, they'd have something else to do." This from a nine-year-old ghetto youth who has four younger brothers and sisters to care for, and who is trying long and hard to deal with everyday "wild ones" —in a jungle we happen to call a "neighborhood" of a particular city.

The real issue, however, for many children, is not Maurice Sendak or various stupid television shows; the issue is the character of family life that is the inheritance, these days, of thousands and thousands of children. Why are children abandoned to hours of no-good television? We are told that *millions* of our children *under thirteen* spend hours at home with no adult present. We are told that more and more children get diagnosed as victims of "child abuse." The teachers I have talked with keep telling me of the pain and sorrow they hear about—broken homes, an increasing crime rate, the constantly accelerating problems of drug and alcohol abuse, each a serious problem in our so-called adult world, to which our children belong, in all their impressionable vulnerability. Guns are everywhere—a measure of endemic fear: of racial war, of possible social and economic collapse, and not least, of assaults and robberies. It is not television that is giving our young a sense of loneliness—giving them, too, a case of the jitters. Nor does television, per se, drive children to despair, to self-loathing, to nasty and brutish behavior toward one another, toward their parents or the neighbors of their parents. I hate to say it, but I feel I should: For some already hurt, bewildered, all-too-anxious, or withdrawn children I have come to know— caught in the middle of one family conflict after another, or caught in the dead-end life of a given ghetto—the television screen, with its banalities and flights of preposterous or mean-spirited fancy, ends up being one of the more reassuring elements in a particular set of circumstances: something there, and relatively reliable, lively, giving.

We who live fairly stable and privileged lives are right to scorn our present-day prevalent "tube junk" —a phrase I heard a boy not yet ten use once. But that same boy consumed "junk food," even as he stared at the very screen he knew offered so little to him. Better that little than the alternative he, sadly, perceived to be his: "nothing to do, no one to be with." Yet another of the latch-key children mentioned above, alone after school in a fancy suburban home, while his parents strive hard through work to keep up with the ever-mounting bills, and when home, strive hard to "unwind." How do they do so? They eat too much; they drink too much; they watch a lot of television. Will the unlikely prospect of a thoroughly reformed attitude toward children's television on the part of our three national networks do much to change that child's essential (existential) situation?

I watch him, I watch other children—and I once more remember the words of William Carlos Williams, as we surveyed together, on a rainy afternoon, the stretches of New Jersey's expanding urban sprawl: "The children come into this world, and their eyes grow wider and wider—until the blows of fate come thick and fast, and the eyes close and stay closed, even though to a casual observer they seem open. The eyes help such people negotiate through one day, then another, but they stop letting much in. There isn't much that's worthwhile *to* let in. The eyes have learned that." So it goes, I fear, for the eyes of all too many children, cast adrift in all too many rooms, as the box gives forth its lights and shadows, its colors, its darting figures coming out of nowhere, leaving abruptly. The eyes gaze, blink, squint, ogle, glance—but do they really even bother to take stock, to behold and discern?

16.

The Guilt Edge

Clark Whelton

G uilt: The small, insistent voice telling you that with a little more effort you could be having a really miserable time.

Guilt. For me it began on May 9, 1961, in a remote and dusty corner of Fort Bliss, Texas. I was watching television in the day room of Company D. The rest of my platoon had trudged off to the mess hall after our evening ritual of watching the cartoon adventures of Huckleberry Hound, but I had stayed to catch the first few minutes of the evening news. The army was buzzing with rumors about American involvement in a place called Vietnam, and I wanted to see if anything was happening that might interfere with my imminent return to civilian life.

But the lead story that night was not about Vietnam, or even about astronaut Alan Shepard, who had grazed the edge of outer space in a suborbital rocket shot four days earlier. Instead, the announcer was talking about someone named Newton Minow. Recently appointed chairman of the Federal Communications Commission by President Kennedy, Minow had delivered a blistering speech to television broadcasters in which he invited them to watch their own programming from sign-on to sign-off.

"You will see," Minow said, "a procession of game shows, violence, audience-participation shows, formula comedies about totally unbelievable families, blood and thunder, mayhem, violence, sadism, murder, western badmen, western good men, private eyes, gangsters, more violence, and cartoons. And, endlessly, commercials—many screaming, cajoling, and offending. And most of all, boredom.''

There was more. Minow acknowledged that a television western draws a larger audience than a symphony, but scolded, "It is not enough to cater to the nation's whims—you must also serve the nation's needs." The thirty-five-year-old former law partner of Adlai Stevenson cut loose with a condemnation that echoed throughout the country. Television, Minow asserted, is a "vast wasteland."

I cringed, besieged by feelings of shame. If television was a vast wasteland, then I, a founding member of the Fort Bliss Huckleberry Hound Society and television fan extraordinaire, was clearly a vast wastrel. I loved it all, the whole Newton Minow hit list. I loved the game shows, the formula comedies, the unbelievable families, the private eyes, gangsters and gunplay, cartoons, cajoling commercials, the works. I can still sing the Mott's applesauce jingle from 1950, and as far as I know I hold the record for continuous contemplation of a test pattern.

But ever since Newton Minow painted a "wasteland" label on my viewing habits, I have been dogged by doubt. Whenever I settle back for a Mary Tyler Moore rerun or another session with "Family Feud," I hear that small voice telling me I am contributing to the decline of Western Civilization, and I feel guilty. I have spent more than a little time examining this curious exercise in self-condemnation, and I know there are millions of others who suffer from the same affliction.

How did a mechanical contrivance like television get cross-wired into the American conscience? Did it really start with Newton Minow? In fact, the origins of television guilt go back a long way, and are probably as old as the medium itself. *New York Times* critic Jack Gould had already taken a swipe at television as early as 1948, when sets had tubes instead of transistors. Gould wrote that children's shows appeared to be a "narcotic" administered by parents, who had learned that plunking junior down in front of the Philco would keep him out of their hair for an hour or two. By calling television a narcotic instead of something that kids enjoy watching, Gould helped to establish a pattern of overkill in television criticism that would largely be delivered via television's major competitor—newspapers.

Very early in the struggle for media domination, the newspaper business showed its fangs: It was the summer of 1950. At the editorial offices of the *New York Journal-American,* flagship paper of the Hearst publishing empire, a sudden meeting was called. Among the handpicked reporters attending that meeting was Atra Baer, daughter of the well-known humor columnist Bugs Baer.

"The editor came right to the point," Baer recalls. "A message had been received from William Randolph Hearst, the chief himself. It seems that Mr. Hearst was very worried about television, especially about the 'deleterious' effect that it might be having on the American public. So a team of *Journal-American* reporters was assigned to canvass the New York City area and come up with some quotes—particularly from mothers—that would focus on the 'bad effects' of television."

Orders in hand, the reporters fanned out. Atra Baer was sent to a nearby suburb, where she asked the requisite questions in the requisite way: "Madam, are you worried about the harmful effect television is having on your children's eyesight? Are you concerned about the harmful effect television has on your children's reading habits?" The sought-after answers were easily obtained, and a story on the "dangers of television" was easily written. At that time there were Hearst papers in every section of the country.

Merrill Panitt, the editor of *TV Guide,* remembers just how effective antitelevision journalism was.

"In our early issues," Panitt says, "we constantly had to answer all the negative stories circulating about television. We ran articles reassuring our readers that no, television is not bad for your eyes; no, television is not bad for your back; no, television does not cause cancer, and it certainly doesn't cause constipation."

Given the newspapers' antipathy toward radio, their alarm at the arrival of television—radio with pictures—can be imagined. The antagonism even extended into press conferences, where newspaper reporters often salted their questions with expletives ("Senator, don't bullshit us, when the hell is Congress going to pass that goddamn tax bill?") so that broadcasters, whose vocabularies are sanitized by their license oligations, couldn't run the footage on the air. When naughty language didn't do the trick, light plugs were pulled, doors were slammed, and coughing epidemics broke out whenever a television reporter asked a question.

"It worked for a while," says a former newspaper reporter who admits to a minor career in sabotage. "But we could see who was winning the war. Politicians wouldn't even let a press conference begin until the cameras arrived."

Newspapers grudgingly accepted the inevitable. The immense popularity of television stars such as Milton Berle and Ed Sullivan had helped to sell millions of sets, and the daily papers had to give their readers what they wanted. Bans against television listings were dropped, even though many papers quietly decided that television coverage deserved to be crammed in with the comics or buried deep inside. This snobbery toward television still exists today. A reporter who worked for *The New York Times* in the 1970s recalls an editor saying that the *Times* would not "debase" its culture section with television news. Television reporting was—and still is—relegated to the back pages.

However, it was in the area of television criticism that newspapers made their biggest dent in the competition. Syndicated columnists like John Crosby specialized in scathing reviews of television programs, reviews implying not only that certain shows were inferior, but that television itself was a medium only a lowbrow could love. Although theater critics were expected to love the theater, and dance and movie critics to revere those art forms, television critics were often people who disdained television.

At the center of this conflict between newspapers and television was a life-or-death struggle. Publishers were well aware that someone who gets his nightly news from the tube is less likely to buy an evening paper. Even before television went on the air, newspapers had been fighting for survival. Dozens of double barreled logotypes *(Post-Dispatch, Herald Tribune)* revealed the many newspaper mergers inspired by the fear of bankruptcy. Fresh competition from television gave newspapers the shudders, especially in large cities where the new medium flourished.

On a national basis, however, there was little reason to fear that television would undermine American literacy. Official figures reveal that the United States had only nine fewer daily papers in 1980 than there were in 1950, and circulation had climbed by more than eight million.

Nevertheless, enemies of television were ever on the alert. In 1963, psychologists claimed to have discovered a "TV Syndrome," which supposedly made kids cranky if they were overexposed to the tube. In the seventies, reports indicated that by the time they reached first grade, television-watching children had spent an average of 5,000 hours in front of the set. A variety of social problems now began to be blamed on television. Low reading scores? College Board scores taking a tumble? Crime and vandalism on the rise? Blame television. And let's not forget the recent news from Tulsa Central Academy in Oklahoma. When English teacher John Zannini's seventh grade class heard that President Reagan had been shot, most of the class cheered. Mr. Zannini blamed it on television.

Television has been subjected to constant scorn and sniping by critics who would have you believe that unless you were watching a show introduced by Alistair Cooke, you had no taste at all. Writer Richard Schickel summed it up this way:

"Television criticism, especially that which aspires to the broad scale and the theoretical, has become, in recent years, little more than a branch of the ecology movement. The brightly glowing box in the corner of the living room is perceived by those who write sober books and Sunday newspaper articles about it as a sort of smoking chimney, spilling God knows what brain-damaging poisons not only into the immediate socio-political environment, but also, it is predicted, loosing agents whose damage may not become apparent to us for decades to come."

In the short run, however, the damage done by snobbish criticism of television is very apparent. America may be the only country in the world where people actually feel guilty about watching. Unfortunately, it is very easy to bully the average American on matters of culture and taste. This vulnerability probably dates back to colonial days, when most settlers were too busy surviving to give much thought to gracious living. All that was refined and cultured arrived on packet boats from Europe—which to a considerable extent is still true today—and Americans became accustomed to taking orders on questions of taste, anxious to be accepted by the rest of the world. Newton Minow betrayed this anxiety in his "wasteland" speech when he asked: "What will people of other countries think of us when they see our western badmen and good men punching each other in the jaw, in between the shooting?"

I can answer that question. American television is very popular throughout the world, where most people consider it a source of entertainment, not of guilt. I once stayed at a small hotel in Barcelona where the only regulation was: "Never interrupt the manager when he's watching "Sea Hunt" or "Have Gun Will Travel." When Americans assigned to a NATO air base in Iceland broadcast old "I Love Lucy" tapes, the show became the number one hit in nearby Reykjavik. In England, where television is a popular pastime, viewers watch anything and everything without apology. But here at home it's a different story. Americans are plagued by guilt for enjoying television.

There is, for example, the guilt parents impose on children. Michael J. Arlen, television critic for *The New Yorker,* compared this parental harassment to the guilt-mongering and mythologizing frequently surrounding the subject of masturbation. "Authorities, for example, such as parents and educators, suggest that it may cause vague harm . . . though generally speaking there are rarely any visible signs of ill effects." Instead of encouraging children to develop good judgment about their television habits, parents sometimes taint the whole topic with implications of moral failure by those who watch any television at all. The result is not less television viewing, but subterfuge and feelings of guilt when the set is on.

There is also the vague fear that the tube is wasting your time. You spent all day Saturday watching a "Gilligan's Island" festival, and when you're through you discover that the lawn still isn't mowed. And you feel guilty. Obviously, television offers extraordinary opportunities for wasting time. There is nothing easier than turning on a set, and if television is being used as an excuse for avoiding other duties, then guilt feelings are probably justified.

Then, of course, there is status guilt, the least logical variety of television angst. You prefer "M*A*S*H" to Mendelssohn, but you're afraid the neighbors will find out. You've read critic John Mason Brown's quip that television is "chewing gum for the eyes," and now you deny that you like to chew gum. Status guilt can be a serious problem; however, it will help to know that those who regularly demean television do so out of a need to feel unique. It's easy to be snobbish about the theater, restaurants, clothes, or literature, because status seekers can always claim to have been the first to discover a new play, bistro, fashion, or book. Television, which reaches everyone at the same time, offers little in the way of snob appeal. The viewer can only claim to have done what everyone else in the country could have done if he had turned on his set, and there is no distinction at all in such a boast. Now and then a "cult" show like "Mary Hartman, Mary Hartman" will come along, but as soon as enough people tune in, the snobs tune out and turn up their noses at anyone who doesn't do the same.

The fact that most television guilt has no basis in reality does not mean that television is without flaws. However, it takes more than one generation to shape and refine an innovation so powerful and revolutionary, and we're learning all the time. As for those who agree that television is indeed a vast wasteland, and that those who watch it deserve to be burdened by guilt, I suggest that the world before television was not exactly paradise. Boredom, loneliness, ignorance—these and other social ills have been around for a long time.

From the window of the Company D day room where I watched "Huckleberry Hound," I could see the distant summit of Guadalupe Peak, ninety miles away across the high plains desert. Ninety miles of sand and chaparral. Ninety miles of nothing. But the Company D television set brought the world a little bit closer. Anybody who has seen a real "vast wasteland" will tell you that television is a vast relief.

17.

Why the New Right Is All Wrong about Prime Time

Walter Karp

According to a much-discussed book called *Post-Conservative America,* fascism will soon be menacing the United States, inflicted upon us by what author Kevin Phillips calls "populist lower-middle-class conservatism." This debased conservatism, he argues, manifests itself in hatred of the rich and the poor, in hunger for a Leader, in the belief that "it might be necessary to use force to restore the American way of life." This political force, as detected by Phillips, shows a marked proclivity for "cultural and moral traditionalism" and a sharp appetite for "nationalist pride and grandeur." Its political triumph will produce, he says, "a peculiarly American authoritarianism, apple-pie authoritarianism" —the bitter fruit of lower-middle-class America's jingoism, its disillusion with Reagan, and its lawless moral bigotry.

My first thought on reading Phillips's prognostication was that American conservatives have been predicting rabble-inspired tyrannies since July 4, 1776. My second thought was the rueful admission that this, in truth, is no happy time in America. Popular frustration, disillusion, and "traditionalist" reaction are not merely the bogeys of a timid elitist. They are real enough, so real that I decided to do what I had not done since Uncle Miltie was the king of video: sit down and watch attentively the ten or so most popular prime-time television series (soaps, sitcoms, mysteries) of the 1981-1982 season. If there was such a thing as "populist lower-middle-class conservatism," it seemed to me that nothing would reveal its nature more clearly than "Dallas," "M*A*S*H," "The Dukes of Hazzard," et al. This is true because you cannot tell popular stories, and maintain their popular rank against stiff competition, unless you affirm with dogged devotion and perfect pitch the moral and political sentiments of millions upon millions of viewers, the bulk of whom Kevin Phillips would surely describe as "lower-middle-class." What makes most of the top dozen television dramas almost unbearably insipid is also what makes them an opinion poll incomparably more subtle than the clumsy questionnaires of the professional pollsters.

Take the quite complex issue of "moral traditionalism" that, to give Kevin Phillips his due, runs rampant through almost every hit show that I watched. In "One Day at a Time," Mrs. Romano's daughter elopes to Las Vegas; in due course she is persuaded to return home for a "real wedding" that will give joy to grandma. Matrimonial ritual triumphs over footloose romance. In "Alice," Mel Sharples, owner of the diner, decides to have his nose surgically improved. Lying in the hopsital, however, he suddenly recalls that his uncomely, banana-shaped nose is just like his late father's. "It's a Sharples nose," says Mel in a sudden surge of pride. Cosmetic surgery is canceled as filial piety triumphs over personal vanity.

Moral and cultural traditionalism are ever victorious, but the main point, the politically significant point, is that they are never shown triumphing over any particular enemy. They are pitted against no faction, group, creed, or individual bent on subverting old-fashioned morality. Moreover, on at least half a dozen hit shows the prevailing moral conservatism is cast in a strikingly genial mode. This is done by pitting old-fashioned ways and precepts against modern-day social novelties. The main novelty in prime time is the irregular household. Alice is a divorcée with a teenage son; Mrs. Romano is a divorcée who raises a college-age daughter and a young boy who is not even a kinsman. Archie in "Archie Bunker's Place" is an aged widower who lives with a teenage niece and her female cousin. The family in "Too Close for Comfort" lives in two separate apartments in the same two-story house: the parents upstairs, the two daughters and their cousin below. In "Three's Company," the household is extremely irregular, consisting of two nubile young women and a young man, linked at the outset by no ties of family, friendship, or sexual intimacy.

The irregular household is obviously a way of epitomizing a whole slew of social novelties that America has experienced during the past twenty turbulent years. What are the consequences? The answer is, there aren't any. The divided family in "Too Close for Comfort" suffers no real division at all. When the father reads his will aloud to the assembled household, everyone starts complaining just like any old-time, old-fashioned family would. Alice renounces her "big break" as a touring singer in order to raise her son properly. The household relationship in "Three's Company," which consists chiefly of suppressed desires and unavowed affections, forces the three roommates into an endless succession of fibs and white lies. That a false position breeds falsity is the traditionalist moral principle of the program and the source of what little humor it generates.

The theme running through all these irregular-household shows is that, despite social novelty, the old moral verities always triumph, which is another way of saying that novelty and change are not so threatening after all. A century's worth of social thinkers and historians have been trying their best to persuade us that nothing ever remains the same, but the plain people of America, invincibly anti-intellectual, still believe that nothing important ever really changes. In this they would agree with Rudyard Kipling, who once said, "The gods of the copybook maxims always return." That confident faith is not the sort of debased and frightened traditionalism that sweeps tyrants into power.

Traditional precepts, moreover, must stand the test of experience. They are not adhered to slavishly, for Americans still possess the old, bumptious habits of freedom. The essential comedy of Archie Bunker, for example, consists in his utter inability to distinguish between old-fashioned prejudice— "all boys is animals" —and old-fashioned common sense. Experience, come upon him unbidden, makes the distinction for him, or at any rate, for the viewers. In one fine episode Archie persuades his good friend and neighbor to accept as a lodger an ailing man who is patently deranged. The man is a Republican, a businessman, and an Elk—so Archie, always blinded by hand-me-down doctrines, is certain he's sound as a bell. After turning everyone's life into a nightmare, the wretched man dies right before the two friends' eyes. In the final scene Archie's friend grows maudlin thinking about his late lodger's dying without any family at hand. Archie, however, will have none of that. Old-fashioned common sense tells him that his pal's mournful pity is but self-pity ill-disguised, although he had to learn the hard way that an Elk can be a madman ill-disguised.

Experience separates what is valuable and what is dross in the mish-mash of verities and follies that make up the cultural and moral tradition. In "One Day at a Time," Schneider, the aging, amorous janitor, takes up with a twenty-two-year-old girl, much to the Romano family's dismay. Hoping to placate them, he begins spouting a half-dozen variations on that most common of popular American delusions: that aging is largely an illusion. "You're only as old as you feel," insists Schneider. "It's not the clock on the wall that counts. It's the clock inside your heart." It will not take long before life with a twenty-two-year-old girl teaches Schneider the painful truth that growing old, alas, is not illusion.

Since experience distinguishes what is true from what is false in the moral tradition, bigotry—the refusal to learn from experience—is looked upon as the very prince of follies, or worse. It does not protect the cultural and moral traditions. It weakens them. In the moral order affirmed by the prime-time hit shows (an order that can safely be called "populist lower-middle-class conservatism"), bigotry and traditionalism do not work hand in glove, as Kevin Phillips assumed. They appear as antagonists.

An episode of "The Love Boat" gave sharp form to this moral precept in the story of the identical twin sisters who make the cruise on a single ticket, each of them taking turns appearing in public. One sister is looking for romance. The other is an avowed misanthrope determined to despise and repel all men. In a word, she is a bigot; by any traditional moral reckoning, she is a moral subversive as well, for humans, we all know, were born to mate. What cures her are the comical consequences flowing from the heated affair that develops between her sister and the ship's doctor. Whenever he sees the man-hating twin taking her share of the cruise, he rushes forth and woos her ardently. Icy stares, pursed lips, rigid posture, harsh words—none of the devices this young lady uses to repel men can repel the doctor. He is puzzled, but persistent beyond anything the man-hating twin has ever had to cope with. In due course she embraces the doctor and abandons her life-blighting creed. Experience rescues tradition by stamping out the subversive power of bigotry.

The separation of traditionalism and bigotry may not seem, at first glance, especially profound or significant. Neither does the larger moral code of which that separation forms a conspicuous part. Indeed, the moral virtues that the prime-time hit shows affirm and celebrate are singularly unheroic. Honor, glory, self-sacrifice, renunciation, devotion to harsh duty, adherence to unpopular principle—these play almost no part in the moral world of the prime-time shows. The Duke boys in "The Dukes of Hazzard" valiantly foil the greedy schemes of Boss Hogg, but only to protect their family. Beyond that they seem to have no more public spirit than the village idiot. Thomas Magnum of "Magnum P.I." is one of the few figures in the noble private eye tradition who is not represented as a shopworn Galahad tackling the world's corruption single-handed. On the contrary, he is the friend of a man so rich and powerful that the very mention of his name opens doors Sam Spade would have had to pry loose with a jimmy and Jim Rockford with a complicated lie.

The chief moral virtues celebrated in the prime-time hits are sweetly modest ones: tolerance, forgiveness ("we all make mistakes, don't we?"), helpfulness ("what are friends for?"), and kindliness. One episode of "Alice," quite typical, was spent showing Alice letting down a teenage admirer as painlessly as possible. Half the hit shows on television depend for their popularity on an audience in love with kindliness, thoughtfulness, and decency. Whatever threatens these virtues—arrogance and self-importance, for example—is always fair game on prime time. Much of the moral charm of "M*A*S*H" lies in its utterly convincing demonstration that even in a wartime army, candor and kindness need never yield an inch to military hypocrisy, martial cant, and the arrogance of rank—or even military obedience, if it comes to that. Of "nationalist pride and grandeur" there is no sign whatever on the prime-time shows I watched. There's no grandeur of any kind.

It would be easy enough to deride a moral code so limited and undemanding that it makes neighborliness the highest good. It would be a mistake to do so, however, for the real significance of that code is not moral but political. It is the moral code of liberty and democracy; its object is to protect democracy and liberty from harm. The neighborly virtues that form the prime-time moral code—the willingness to help, the willingness to forgive, the determination to consider the other person's feelings—stand as a popular bulwark against tyranny. This is because a tyrant, as de Tocqueville long ago pointed out, does not care if his subjects hate him as long as they dislike each other. The great worth of the neighborly virtues is that they safeguard mutual respect, the thoughtful regard in which fellow citizens hold each other simply because they are fellow citizens. The great value of mutual respect is that it enables free people to act together in great public affairs and so foil the lawless designs of would-be tyrants and ruling cabals. Without such mutual respect, no constitution could safeguard our liberties.

That the televised moral code is deeply political the makers and viewers of prime-time television seem to understand clearly enough, though perhaps in a wordless, intuitive way. This is reflected in the two most striking features of the shows I watched: the determination to celebrate traditional morality without scoring off of a social enemy, and the emphatic insistence that bigotry is no friend of traditional morality. The explanation for this seems clear enough. We live in dark and frustrating times; we have lived through rapid and painful social changes. It is now, most of all, that mutual respect needs special protection. It is as if the great body of the American people were determined not to become the lawless bigots Kevin Phillips expects us to be. The moral code of prime-time television reflects the political determination not to lose the bulwark of our liberty.

Because it is a code of political morality, the prime-time moral code mirrors, too, the American people's enduring love of equality, which figured largely in almost every prime-time show I watched. Commonly it takes the form of equal relations between ostensible unequals: Mel and his waitresses; the Romanos and the janitor; the Harts and their factotum Max on "Hart to Hart"; the Duke boys and the Hazzard County powers; everyone on "M*A*S*H" regardless of rank. What levels the inequalities between employer and employee, master and servant, governor and governed, officer and enlisted man is, of course, the counterforce of equality deriving from citizenship.

In the moral code of prime time, egalitarianism is always a mark of goodness. The unforced, unfailing respect the Harts show to those poorer, weaker, and less lucky than they is clearly meant to be their signal virtue. To the viewers it gives welcome reassurance that the possession of every material blessing need not undercut the equality of citizens. To hate the rich as such forms no part of the prime-time moral code. Only when the very rich deny the fellowship of citizens do they bring moral odium on themselves. What marks Mrs. Channing of "Falcon Crest" as wicked is her arrogant assertion that family "tradition" takes precedence over mere, stupid, "equality." To sneer at the Declaration of Independence is an act of intolerable impiety to the majority of "populist lower-middle-class conservatives"; such an attitude will never bring fascism in its train. The "neo-conservatives" who pretend that it will do not fear fascism, they merely hate equality. The same popular conservatism (as opposed to neo-conservatism) makes J.R. Ewing of "Dallas" America's favorite villain. He is inequality incarnate. Every time he unleashes his personal, lawless, and utterly irresponsible power, he dashes our ancient hopes for a republic of equals. Every time he destroys somebody's self-respect by reducing him to a hapless pawn, he does violence to the deepest meaning of equality in America.

That "all men are created equal" has never meant that all people are alike. The proposition is not refuted by noting that Mr. Jones is five inches taller than Mr. Smith. What it does mean, fundamentally, is that no one is ever entitled to reduce another to a mere means: No master can treat his servant as if he were only a servant; no government can treat the governed as if they merely performed social functions. How well Americans understand this (as the Reaganites are beginning to learn) is neatly attested by an episode of "The Love Boat" that offered three variants on the theme of equality violated by turning people into means. One subplot concerned a long-grieving widow who falls in love with an amiable professor the moment she sets foot on the ship. The second involves a penniless Lothario who persuades an oil heiress that he's a Riviera swell. The third concerns a young woman's determination to bear a genetically well-endowed child by seducing a handsome, healthy, intelligent pro football quarterback. The subplots thicken quickly. The heiress discovers that her glib suitor is a professional fortune hunter. The football star refuses to be reduced to a chromosome supplier. The professor discovers that the widow loves him because he resembles her late husband. All three have been reduced to means, their self-respect badly marred. Not until equality is established between each of the three pairs can happy endings ensue. Unless we recognize the requirements of equality, the whole system of mutual respect is menaced.

This is political understanding of no small order, although Americans possess it by the saving light of intuition, for on the face of it there is no reason why Americans should have any political understanding at all. We are systematically miseducated

18.

Texas:
A Giant State of Mind

Horace Newcomb

One hundred and fifty years ago, people wrote "GTT" over the doorways of busted-out post-war rent farms in Mississippi, Alabama, and Georgia. That meant the family had "Gone to Texas." They piled everything worth taking onto a two-mule wagon and headed west. The people were after cotton and cattle. And land. The oil came later, much of it from under land that was fit for neither cows nor plows, land that had already changed hands more than once by the time it was drilled.

Today they come from Los Angeles and New York; they come in comfort, on the big jets, first class—high rollers, ready to buddy up with the down-home types. Taxiing into the gigantic horseshoes of Dallas-Fort Worth Regional Airport, they already sport the boots and hats, boutique items bought in little side-street shops in fashionable neighborhoods back home.

They've come to scout locations or to film some title sequences and "establishing shots." Or they've come just for the fun of it, to see what it's all about. They'll meet the rich folks with Hollywood connections, talk to the mayor, eat some barbecue. They'll hop in a pickup and wheel down to "Yewston" to see Gilley's and the Galleria, listen to a little music, cuss the heat, and head for home two days later. The very least the new travelers hope for is a good television pilot, something that blends stereotype and audience expectation, glamour and violence, high stakes and low-down loving.

It's residuals they're farming now, the gleam of syndication shining in the vice-presidential glance like hope in the eye of a forty-acre farmer. "GTT" still works. Now it means— "Get Texas Television."

Because of the unexpected success of "Dallas," Texas is hot. *Time* doesn't do covers on subjects that aren't. And while nobody in Los Angeles or New York knows how to start a trend, they certainly do know how to spot one. Quickly then, in every stage of production, come the copies. "Texas," the daytime version of "Dallas," brings the same soap-opera license to old topics of social intrigue, class strife, financial chicanery, and sexual confusion. With marvelous bravado this show moves into such topical areas as Middle Eastern revolution and petroleum politics, while keeping regional roots on the surface with such lines as, "If I had to move off this ranch I guess I would die." "Knots Landing" ties "Dallas" to Southern California with familial ropes, but little more than random accents remain. "Flamingo Road" left Texas for Florida, where flesh and sweat are supposed to be in equal supply.

What are we to make of this sudden run of "y'alls," these "ma'ams," and "Daddys"? These fanciful, often stereotypical, and sometimes exploitative images have seized the public's imagination—highbrow, lowbrow—in England and Nigeria, all around the world. The audience's incredible involvement has a lot to do with the show's exquisitely fortuitous casting. Who could have planned the success of Larry Hagman's grin or of Victoria Principal's testy stride? Even greater contributions to the show's success were the spread of country music and the popularity of crossover performers like Dolly Parton and outlaws like Willie Nelson. Chicago wore boots and the Lone Star Cafe was a New York hit before we had the new television Texans. Even the Cowboys, called "America's Team," show striking similarities to "Dallas." Like Miss Ellie waiting for a phone call, Tom Landry paces the sidelines in tense anticipation, and the Dallas Cowboys' bouncy, sexy cheerleaders give the younger Southfork women lessons in how to dress for breakfast.

"Trend" is too mild a way to explain television's country fixation. "Dallas" and the other shows—*Urban Cowboy* and the country music movies, Burt Reynolds as hero-hick, even Sheriff Lobo, "The Dukes of Hazzard," and the cartoon characters who hang around Flo's café—tap a far deeper source in American entertainment. The West and the South, and now the new hybrid, the Sunbelt, have always served as a mirror on which the image-merchants project characters who never existed, the cowboys, hillbillies, bandits, and dumb sheriffs. Their actions are performed within the broad limits of the imagination, rarely bounded by the average person's experience. Still, they amuse and thrill us, *and* they seem familiar. We have heard it before but never in so appropriately contemporary a manner. These characters are talking to us about ourselves, and their words come from some of popular culture's most powerful and appealing language. What we get is a sense of place, of tradition, and of true character. And we like what we hear because qualities are in very short supply these days.

For the most part television is as devoid of any real sense of place as a theme park. While most critics think that this is because everything is filmed in California, the visual aspects actually have little influence on our *sense* of place. Reference to a regional food, a touch of what the audience thinks of as an accurate accent, and the mood is set. A sense of place must be evoked, not duplicated visually. This is why "Kojak" was better at place than "The Mary Tyler Moore Show." Jump-cut titles that take us around a city do little to evoke its mood if the immediate action doesn't follow through.

Southern shows have been best at developing this quality. "The Beverly Hillbillies" traded continually on the premise that the family had moved from *some*place to *no* place and that it was genuinely disturbed by the fact. "The Waltons" managed, with voice, theme, and historical reference, to plant itself in the minds of viewers as actually representing the mountain communities of Virginia.

"Dallas" and the new Sunbelt series are superb at creating this quality, weaving a texture of place that feels familiar. We've seen the huge swagger, the openness to stranger and friend alike. We've heard the loud, familiar voices, ringing as if everything is a celebration. But we've also seen the sinister threat that comes when the eyes narrow and the voices drop to a whispering intensity. We know all this from John Wayne's drawl, James Arness's stance, the soft thunder of "When you call me that, smile," even from Lyndon Johnson's remembered boasts.

These are the evocative cues. Their real importance is found in qualities that accompany them, telling us that this is a place of confrontation, of testing, of possible violence. The potential for failure is strong, matched only be the sense of possibility. Men and women are measured here daily, and threatened frequently. It is an old and complex dream world in which one must gamble and fight repeatedly to hold on to what he has.

And when Texas is involved, there is always the lust for empire. In history and fiction the state has lured visionaries, politicians, scoundrels, outcasts, missionaries, and entrepreneurs. There was supposed to be enough for them all. But empires call for emperors, emperors become despots, and the dream curdles.

Played small, this is the plight of the gunfighter. Reputation established, he waits now for every puny fool who wants to bring him down. The best examples are in epics like *Red River.* John Wayne, as Tom Dunson, builds his vast ranch from nearly nothing, only to be defeated by a failure of nerve when he is threatened by financial ruin and the manhood of his figurative son. In a way this Texas story is a microcosm, not just for the West, but for the whole country. Cursed and blessed with grand dreams and vast land, we've spent decades trying to remain pure while making the big kill. From the very early westerns through the work of Ford and Hawkes, to films like *Giant, Hud,* and *Urban Cowboy,* we live it out over and over again with our tainted heroes.

What "Dallas" has done—and it counts in large measure for the show's success—is to transfer these old western meanings to a new and different world, to the Dallas of express highways and sunning skyscrapers. The old shows began with the stagecoach topping the horizon. Now we swoop over the scurrying cars in a helicopter, carrying the horizon with us. We sense that the barbecues and lonesome music mask a deadly seriousness. The shoot-outs have merely been transferred to the boardrooms, and when we saw the brothers W. Herbert and Nelson Bunker Hunt bluff Congress on the evening news we understood them better because we know J.R.

But it would be a big mistake to define the new West or the success of "Dallas" solely in terms of these regional characteristics. Eventually tradition tamed the frontier and checked rampant opportunism.

In "Dallas," tradition begins at home. Throughout the show we swing from office to ranch, restaurant to dining room, boardroom to den. Family is the second powerful attraction of the show. As we Texans sometimes say, "How's ya Mama'n'em?"

Thank goodness Miss Ellie didn't marry Digger Barnes. Despite his protestations to the contrary, not even the passionate love of this good woman would have kept him from becoming a whiny old drunk. In choosing Jock she chose the sunrise of a dynasty. She holds the family together with those crinkly-eyed smiles and bosomy embraces. Jock may not have understood it all, but when one of the boys or girls offended his wife, or what she stands for, he came down with both boots. Actually, like all good parents, Miss Ellie wants the best for her kids, and also like most parents she spends a fair amount of time worrying about them. That's part of the tradition.

Again, the real genius of the show emerges in the tension of transferring those old values to the inhabitants of the new West. For all the younger Ewings, their spouses, friends, and assorted lovers, these traditions are the backdrop against which they play out their own frantic struggles for stability, happiness, and success. They believe in the old ways, but they don't know how to make them work in a time and place where money and power dominate. Tradition makes Pam feel inferior, but it also drives her to search for her own personal identity. For Sue Ellen and Lucy, tradition threatens freedom. Both are trapped, and to escape they must behave badly. To the old people, then, tradition is part of a rich existence and full of meaning. To the young ones it is merely part of the air they breathe. And to J.R. it is a tool.

Utterly realistic in the show's fictional world, J.R. at once embodies the sense of place and sneers at it. He believes in tradition and family, perhaps more than anyone else, and he uses them to keep Bobby in line and Sue Ellen on a string. Dynasty is what he wants and he will go to any length to obtain it. There is no contradiction in character when J.R. tenderly holds his infant son. He is holding his world together until his son can take over. That is J.R.'s one and only business, hobby, dream, and burden.

He is the third great feature of "Dallas," made possible in part by the other two: sense of place and the idea of tradition. Without such texture he would be a caricature. Hagman also helps to prevent this with small actions. His face disintegrates when someone discovers one of his schemes, his anger pours out briefly before he regains control of Sue Ellen. He hurries from his call girl because he finds no real satisfaction.

As a result, television has its most developed character since Archie Bunker, and the two are much alike. Both are obstinate, intent on blundering through the world as if they were utterly sure of their intentions and actions. All the while we know that they remain on the verge of failure and defeat. They appeal to us as much for their weaknesses as for their strengths. We like to know that behind their facades our villains are touchy and vulnerable.

J.R. blends the old West and new, inevitably winning battles by using old ways. He pushes civility to the limits, strains every family tie, every sign of love, overlooking basic morality, the law, and business ethics. If there is something to grab, J.R. grabs it.

In this way he is much like the prototypical "Good Old Boy." What is marvelous about that term is that many of us truly desire to be "Old" and to be a "Boy." We want to behave rambunctiously and at the same time be taken seriously, getting adult responsibility in the arenas of money, sex, and power. Therefore in his action, the Good Old Boy demands to be honored, and pleads for approval.

More than anything else, more than money or even power, J.R. longed for his father's approval. Without this he would have nothing of true value to pass on to his own son. To receive the nod from Jock, J.R. had to be capable of some flamboyant act, something truly worthy of his father's own exploits. Around this theme many Ewing narratives have unfolded. With its brilliant appropriation of soap opera form, "Dallas," perhaps indefinitely, has postponed resolutions. In such an unending story there is always hope, for J.R. and for us.

The power of "Dallas" lies in this extraordinary accomplishment of the oldest pop-culture trick. It has recycled a cluster of America's most basic images and polished them into a financial success. Probably without knowing it, the show's creators pump nourishment into audience's veins. Their timing is perfect. As a nation we are actually growing older and developing the caution that comes with age. It is a time of decline, of recession and restriction, a time of real trouble. The grand old cities of the East and the Midwest are burdened with financial failure and bitter winters. Small wonder that the Sunbelt flourishes and "Dallas" leads the ratings. Small wonder, too, that J.R. has become a national symbol, replacing the mellower, resigned, saddened Archie Bunker.

A certain political resonance in all of this relates to our recent presidential elections. Carter's success was much like the initial success of "Dallas"; both were exotic. In the new South, the true southern romantic and the cavalier have long since been replaced by the efficient manager. There may have been little of J.R. in Jimmy Carter—but we usually go for the loner, the outsider from the hills that Carter represented. In 1976 he was the only one willing to face down the gang in town. The Sunbelt was promising its old salvation and, for a moment, when Carter's people walked down Constitution Avenue, it was as if the film hero Shane had come back. Now that all seems anachronistic. It didn't work, and like Cooper at the end of the film *High Noon,* Carter packed up his family and rode out. In 1980, the incoming Reagan Administration promised style and power, an understanding of boardroom politics, big money, and smooth deals. At that moment, J.R. and the glamour of high finance were more intriguing to us—offered more—than the gunfighter's purity of mission.

The paradox is obvious. The wheelers and dealers in "Dallas" are all hip-deep in booze, blackmail, and what some folks call illicit sex. Their world has a frightening callousness. It may sound rather offensive to many Reagan supporters, and no doubt the Moral Majority eschews "Dallas" as another example of crumbling values. But for them, as for many voters, the unpleasantness of tawdry glitter and soiled boots are overshadowed by what they see as the Reagan Administration's sense of purpose and will. Maybe we should have anticipated the conservative sweep when J.R., acting on knowledge gained from his private intelligence sources, saved Ewing Oil from the clutch of greedy nationalists. In the face of utter disaster he took action and did what a man had to do. No negotiation. No fine ethical dilemma. That he sold friends out in the process might give momentary pause but for the ruthless clarity of intention. We had already heard of Lone Ranger diplomacy. No wonder "J.R. for President" bumper stickers appeared immediately.

What we see in J.R. is a refusal to give up. He holds on. The grand gestures count, as they always have in the romance of the West and the South. Why else would John Travolta in *Urban Cowboy* need so desperately to ride the bull and ride it better? Why would we thrill to Burt Reynolds' "bandit" character if it were not for his remarkable will?

This is why settlers came to Texas originally, and why "GTT" never needed a translation. This is why we always have westerns in America although they are high-rise, glass-fronted, six-lane concrete westerns. Even if there are old Mercedes hubcaps lying beside the road instead of buffalo chips, we want the old dream. As usual, imagination exceeds experience.

Other shows will try to move in on the territory. Many of them will succeed in capturing one or two of the elements that have

19.

The Season of
the Reagan Rich

Michael Pollan

During the Depression, when people were selling apples, *and factories were still, and guys were jumping out of windows because they had lost everything, people would go to the movies. They loved those glamour pictures . . . showing people driving beautiful cars and women in beautiful gowns, showing that people were still living the glamorous good life.*
>   —Charles Z. Wick, defending
>   the extravagance of the Reagan inauguration.

It has been several years since California millionaire Charles Z. Wick presided over the lavish inaugural of his old friend Ronald Reagan. Limousines and Galanos gowns are now fixtures in Washington, and the economy has not looked so bad since the thirties. Still, Wick's theory that the poor get a vicarious kick from Republican champagne seems only to gain credence as the nation gains poor people. Turn on the television any night and you'll find the eighties version of those "glamour pictures . . . showing people still living the glamorous good life." The rich are always with us, perhaps, but only now have they arrived on television.

Ralph Kramden, Ward Cleaver, Chester Riley, Archie Bunker: American television has traditionally celebrated the common man. Today, however, prime time seems less confident of its old dreams of middle-class utopia. The season of J.R. Ewing, Jonathan

Hart, and Blake Carrington signals a radical change in television's own demographics. Of course, rich people have always surfaced on television—think of Thurston Howell III, or Chatsworth Osborne III—but always on the peripheries, for comic relief or as one-shot villains. Only recently have the wealthy gotten their own shows, and they've made "Dallas," "Dynasty," "Hart to Hart," and "Falcon Crest" four of television's most popular series. But the spectacle of opulence on television is not limited to prime time; lately the news, too, regales us with formal affairs at the White House, the continuing drama of Nancy Reagan's couture, and the First Couple's holiday weekends at Claudette Colbert's or the Annenbergs'. Indeed, the "glamour pictures" of prime time bear an often uncanny resemblance to those of Washington: "Falcon Crest's" icy matriarch could easily be mistaken for Nancy Reagan, and in fact is played by Jane Wyman, the president's first wife.

If proof were needed of the similarities between thirties entertainment and our own, the popularity of a program such as "Hart to Hart" is it. Modeled on the Depression-era film *The Thin Man,* "Hart to Hart" is a genial fantasy about a debonaire "self-made millionaire" and his beautiful wife, who occupy their considerable leisure time with unpaid, freelance sleuthing. When not unraveling mysteries, the Harts consume conspicuously, though not without taste. They tool around Los Angeles in a bright yellow coupe, jet off to romantic retreats, shop on Rodeo Drive, and lavish expensive gifts on one another.

"The rich are different from you and me," Fitzgerald once remarked. Replied Hemingway, "Yeah, they've got more money." Like the plutocrats at the end of a Depression comedy (such as Frank Capra's *It Happened One Night),* the Harts are no different underneath their money and their manners from you and me—which is why they can be so casually egalitarian with their chauffeur Max. In hard times, the Harts bring comforting news, for if the rich are really like us, then possibly we can be like them. The Harts imply that there are still great fortunes to be made in America and, better still, that the "good life" —with all the accoutrements advertised on the commercials—is worth sweating for after all.

But the Harts do not typify the rich on television. Blake Carrington, Angela Channing, and J.R. Ewing, the prototype of them all, are much darker and more complicated figures; indeed, they make one wonder whether the current preoccupation with "the glamorous good life" is as benign as it seems to have been in the thirties. Behind each of their dynasties stretches a lurid history of double-crossings, dirty deals, adulteries, and crushed rivals. The prime-time soaps titillate by exploiting the tested combination of sex, money, and power. But their special appeal lies less in the conventions they follow than in one they flout: These programs lavish attention on the villains whom television typically dispatches in a single episode.

There is something undeniably satisfying about all this villainy. If "Hart to Hart" puts us on an equal footing with the rich, "Dallas," "Dynasty," and "Falcon Crest" give us the satisfaction of feeling superior to them: We can look down on their skewed values and perverted family lives from the high ground of middle-class respectability. When Angela Channing coolly threatens to disinherit her grandson if he won't wed a woman he despises (the marriage would tighten her hold on the valley's wine industry), our own superior respect for love and marriage is confirmed. The prime-time soaps also confirm the suspicion that great wealth and power are predicated on sin and, even more satisfying, don't buy happiness anyway.

These are bland comforts, however, and can't fully account for the popularity of these programs. Probably more important is all that the Ewings, Carringtons, and Channings give us to covet. Most of prime time is bumper to bumper with prosy Chevys and Fords, so it's a luxury to watch Mercedes and Lamborghinis gliding down manicured driveways. The clothes, brand-new in every scene, dazzle, too, although instead of the Galanos's and Adolfos one might expect, television's rich favor a look best described as "Hollywood silk" —those slinky, maximum-cleavage numbers that reveal more about the audience's idea of extravagance than about the tastes of the wealthy.

Indeed, the prime-time soaps do not seem very interested in accurately depicting the details and textures of upper-class American life. Unlike novels about the rich, or even "Masterpiece Theatre," class is scarcely an issue in these shows. Instead of putting the Carringtons or Ewings in any particular relation to society, wealth simply transports them to a dreamy, streamlined realm resembling no real place as much as the facile world of a television commercial, perhaps for a cosmetic or an aperitif.

The rich-people shows also seem to borrow their sense of the good life's tempo from television commercials. Unlike their daytime counterparts, the prime-time soaps go through plots as if they were disposable towels. By swiftly cutting between vignettes, an episode can develop as many as four subplots, normally divided between tales of corporate intrigue for the men in the audience (Cecil Colby plots a raid on Denver Carrington stock), and stories of emotional intrigue for the women (Colby renews his steamy affair with Alexis Carrington). With all these plots and fast cuts, an episode of "Dynasty" flies by like a thirty-second "Reach out and touch someone" spot turned on its head. Not only do the rich on television have more things than ordinary people, they also seem to have more life—conspicuous consumption is evidently not limited to commodities.

But there's more to envy the prime-time rich than their cars and gowns and plotty lives. The Ewings, Carringtons, and Channings play out irresistible fantasies of unbridled personal power, flaunting their freedom from all of the strictures that bind our own lives. Undeterred by price or opinion, they spend their days gratifying their merest wish, whether that involves picking up a mink or wrecking a marriage. When Alexis Carrington decides to get rid of her son's ill-mannered bride, she simply pays the girl enough money to leave Denver permanently. According to television, the rich are exempt from any abiding standards of conduct; they are free to improvise their own rules. This is a world very different from the one portrayed in the thirties films, where the wealthy, stifled by archaic manners, could win freedom only by forsaking their class.

At the Ewings' Southfork, in the Channings' California valley, and in Blake Carrington's Denver, money has loosened the ties of civilization, making for a world of abundant thrills, if few securities. Each of us at one time has wished for a rival's failure, but how many live out that daydream as methodically as J.R. does? In one characteristic scenario, he lures Cliff Barnes into a lucrative oil-well deal, knowing it will force Barnes to borrow cash from his family's business. J.R. doesn't tell Barnes the wells are dry, preferring to watch with undisguised relish as his rival's world comes tumbling down. "My, my," he sympathizes when Barnes comes begging on his knees, "look what a failure you've become."

These cartoonish daydreams of power and freedom have an obvious political significance. Is it only a coincidence that the rise of J.R. Ewing's popularity followed closely on the decline of Jimmy Carter's? At the same time successive crises in energy, the economy, and Iran were paralyzing the Carter Administration,

J.R. extracted Ewing Oil from a Third World quagmire in one brilliant, ruthless stroke, and "J.R. for President" stickers turned up on bumpers across America.

J.R.'s ratings were a tip-off: As the eighties began, Americans had had enough of Jimmy Carter's sober moralizing and dowdy, middle-class tastes. The country was ready for something stronger and more stylish: expediency in foreign policy, glamour in the White House, and an economic recovery propelled by unapologetically self-interested millionaires. As Alexis Carrington and J.R. Ewing are fond of saying, "The ends justify the means."

That ethic, which is getting such a workout today, enjoyed an earlier vogue in this country: It ruled the Old West. It's not surprising that every one of the prime-time soaps is set in the West; Americans have always looked in that direction to fulfill their dreams of individual power and collective renewal. All of these programs are about latter-day cowboys, some in white hats, some in black ones, who come in and get the job done. Evidently grasping the enduring power of these images, the president regularly returns to California, dons a big white cowboy hat, and rides around on a horse.

Indeed, the similarities between the imagery of Reaganism and the prime-time soaps are hard to miss. Like the millionaires who propelled Ronald Reagan into politics—Charles Z. Wick, Justin Dart, the late Alfred Bloomingdale—the rich of prime time are all self-made men who accumulated vast fortunes in the West. As Washington society noted sourly on its arrival, the Reagan crowd is hopelessly *nouveau riche,* deficient in the graces and decorum that distinguish the older families of the East. Certainly Reagan's entourage shares more with the Ewings of Dallas than the Rockefellers of New York.

Television's rich and the Reagan rich also share something more insidious—their nostalgic fantasy of wealth in America. The prime-time soaps and Washington's supply-siders both depict American capitalism as a free-wheeling affair among adventurous entrepreneurs—the Blake Carringtons, Jock Ewings, Angela Channings. Both hark back to a time before the giant corporation and the professional manager. Hannah Arendt once pointed out that people will abide the conspicuous display of wealth in hard times only as long as they are convinced the rich are performing a necessary role in society. They do, according to Reagan and the supply-side soaps; both imply that the American dream of self-made success is alive and might be made well by releasing the frontier instincts of the wealthy from the twin shackles of taxes and regulation.

But already signs of disillusion are visible. Reagan is widely perceived to favor the rich at the expense of everyone else, and, even worse, the rich have failed to deliver on their promise of trickle-down prosperity. Perhaps because we seem constitutionally incapable of anger toward this president, his wife has become a kind of lightning rod for our growing animus. "Falcon Crest," the youngest of the prime-time soaps and last season's only new hit, exploits this phenomenon. In a brilliant impersonation of the First Lady, Jane Wyman pricks all our contradictory feelings about the rich; as with Nancy Reagan, we admire her poise and strength, and despise her as an American Marie Antoinette.

The prime-time soaps make clear that the flip side of envy is resentment. However much we may covet their wealth and power, J.R. Ewing, Angela Channing, and the other supply-side heroes are, as the gossip magazines like to say, people "you love to hate." "Who shot J.R.?" became a momentous national question because there were so many who would gladly have pulled the trigger, including the legions of those we call, for lack of any better word, his "fans." A lot of ugly emotions go into watching these programs, and if they teach anything, it is that our present fascination with the rich and powerful is liable to take an ugly turn. Charles Z. Wick's blithe assumptions about the charms of glamour in high places are only partially correct; he forgets how far it is from Frank Capra's world to Southfork.

20.

Archie Bunker and the Liberal Mind

Christopher Lasch

In the late sixties, advertisers discovered a new market. Surveys told them that the most voracious consumers were now affluent, urban, educated people under the age of thirty-five. In an attempt to reach this audience, the networks began to experiment with programs slightly more sophisticated than "The Beverly Hillbillies," "The Ed Sullivan Show," and "Marcus Welby." After much hesitation, CBS—which had least to lose at the time—introduced Norman Lear's "All in the Family" in January 1971. For the first time, a network had dared to confront its audience with a middle-American antihero who vents the most outrageous opinions, tyrannizes over his wife, and bickers endlessly with his daughter and her husband, who struggle unsuccessfully to overcome his prejudices against blacks, Jews, women, and other "un-American" minorities. Archie Bunker proved so durable a character that he has been with us ever since, in one show or another.

From the start, Archie Bunker became the object of passionate controversy. Did the depiction of his bigotry have the therapeutic effect of dragging a sensitive issue into the open and forcing viewers to confront their own prejudices? Or did it reinforce bigotry by making it respectable? According to Robert Wood, former president of CBS, "All in the Family" helped to "ventilate some of the prejudices and misconceptions in American society today." Many reviewers agreed that "All in the Family" served an "important purpose," even if it offended liberals and other "uptight viewers." A CBS survey of the show's audience indicated that most viewers took it as a satire, not a vindication, of prejudice. But a somewhat more extensive (though still flawed and simplistic) survey, by sociologists Neil Vidmar and Milton Rokeach, concluded that the program probably reinforced prejudice instead of combatting it.

Laura Z. Hobson, author of *Gentlemen's Agreement,* claimed in a 1971 *New York Times* article that "All in the Family" sanitized prejudice and made it socially acceptable. Her vigorous attack on Archie Bunker and his creators captured the indignation of an older generation of liberals appalled by what they saw as an attempt to make bigotry loveable, "to clean it up, deodorize it, make millions of people more comfy about indulging in it." In reply, Norman Lear accused Hobson of underestimating the intelligence of middle Americans, who could be trusted, he insisted, to recognize his work as satirical in its intention. Yet surveys showing that most viewers identified with Archie (even though many of them thought son-in-law Mike got the better of their arguments) strengthened the fear that the program elicited a "sadistic response," as one educator put it, and served "no constructive purpose." (These views and others were collected by Richard P. Adler in a volume entitled *All in the Family: A Critical Appraisal,* published by Praeger.)

Both Archie Bunker and the controversy he has generated tell us a great deal about the liberal mind today. "All in the Family" and "Archie Bunker's Place" implicitly take the position that resistance to social change, failure to "adjust" to change, and fear of change have pathological roots. Lear has argued that Archie Bunker's bigotry rests not on hatred but on the "fear of anything he doesn't understand." Because this fear is irrational, Archie's prejudices cannot be corrected by rational persuasion. Although Mike's arguments always "make sense," according to Lear, while Archie's rebuttals are "totally foolish," Archie can't be decisively defeated by Mike.

Liberals of Laura Hobson's type, convinced that bigotry can be combatted by propaganda depicting it in the most unattractive light, mistakenly see the Archie Bunker programs as a capitulation to popular prejudices. What the programs really seem to say, however, is that prejudice is a disease and that the only way to overcome it, as in psychotherapy, is to bring to light its irrational origins. " 'All in the Family' simply airs [prejudice]," according to Lear, "brings it out in the open, has people talking about it."

The series seems to have been influenced, at least indirectly, by the theory of "working-class authoritarianism," which has played an important part in the thinking of social scientists and members of the helping professions ever since the late forties. According to this widely accepted interpretation, prejudice, ethnocentricity, and intolerance of ambiguity originate in the authoritarian child-rearing practices allegedly characteristic of working-class families. Archie Bunker has all the traits commonly attributed to the authoritarian husband and father. Lear's dramatization of Bunker's anti-Semitism, racism, male chauvinism, and xenophobia shares with the sociological literature on authoritarianism a tendency to reinterpret class issues in therapeutic terms and to reduce political conflicts to psychological ones. It ignores the possibility that "middle Americans" have legitimate grievances against society, legitimate misgivings about what is called social progress.

Yet the few gains that have been made in race relations, desegregation, and women's rights have usually been achieved at the expense of the white working-class male. His anger cannot be understood, therefore, as a purely psychological reaction; it has an important political basis. His dislike of liberals, moreover, springs not so much from "anti-intellectualism" or ethnocentricity as from the realistic perception that working-class values are the chief casualties of the "cultural revolution" with which liberalism has increasingly identified itself. With his unsentimental but firm commitment to marriage and family life, his respect for hard work and individual enterprise, and his admittedly old-fashioned belief that people should accept the consequences of their actions, the working-class male rightly regards himself as a forgotten man in a society increasingly dominated by the permissive, therapeutic morality of universal understanding. He sees himself, not without reason, as the victim of bureaucratic interference, welfarism, and sophisticated ridicule. Lacking any real political choices, he sometimes vents his anger in an ill-considered politics of right-wing moralism. But it is well known that many of the same voters who supported George Wallace also supported Robert Kennedy (and in any case the Wallace vote did not by any means come exclusively from the working class).

"All in the Family" and "Archie Bunker's Place" make no attempt to depict the political basis of working-class prejudice, or even to capture the complexity of the attitudes it dramatizes. The programs reduce a complex historical experience to the single issue of "bigotry," which they then approach as a form of pathology.

But what is true of Norman Lear's famous series is equally true of the commentary they have inspired. Both critics and defenders agree that the "disease" of bigotry is the important issue; they differ only on the question of whether Lear's talking-cure may be worse than the disease itself. Thus historian John Slawson (after stating flatly that "bigotry is sickness") argues that Archie Bunker brings out the worst in his fans. Quoting political sociologist Seymour Martin Lipset on working-class authoritarianism, Arthur Asa Berger (author of *The TV-Guided American*) congratulates "All in the Family" for demolishing the "myth of the common man." But whereas the myth upholds the working man as the salt of the earth, Lipset, and Norman Lear, suggest that he is actually a bigot, endowed with attitudes "to make you shudder." Like many critics, however, Berger would prefer a more straightforward and unambiguous condemnation of Archie Bunker and his kind. Lear's comedy, he thinks, embodies a kind of pornography of prejudice, ridiculing ethnocentric attitudes but at the same time inviting the viewer to find titillation in their frank expression.

There may be some justice in Berger's charge that "All in the Family" delivers a "double payoff": "We enjoy the ethnic humor yet feel superior to it." But instead of asking whether such ridicule serves a useful social purpose, commentators might better ask whether anything of artistic value is served by appealing so consistently to an audience's sense of superiority. Laura Hobson considered the program "elitist" because only well-educated liberal intellectuals would feel superior to Archie Bunker. Lear, noting that Hobson had unwittingly exposed her own elitism, replied in effect that liberal attitudes are now so widely diffused (at least among the younger viewers he was trying to reach) that almost anyone would feel superior to such an antiquated buffoon. When it nevertheless turned out that many viewers do identify with Archie, even though they do not necessarily endorse all his opinions, this fact—instead of prompting speculation about the complexity of the emotional response elicited by the series—simply reinforced the fear that it might have undesirable social effects.

Yet art of any merit to some extent transcends the immediate intentions of its creators. Although "All in the Family" and "Archie Bunker's Place" invite ridicule of their hero, as their defenders contend, the programs also seem to evoke a more complicated response. For one thing, these programs—especially the original series—deal with emotionally resonant themes of family life. In one survey of "All in the Family's" audience, the children in a working-class family told an interviewer that their mother, like Edith Bunker, mediated generational arguments. Many middle-class mothers could doubtless say the same thing.

Part of the Bunker household's appeal to a more "sophisticated" audience, I suspect, lies in its power to evoke reminders of ethnic neighborhoods and ethnic cultures that the program's upwardly mobile young viewers have left behind in their climb into the "new class." In the conflict between Archie Bunker and his son-in-law, who rises during the course of the series from a Polish working-class background to a university teaching position, "All in the Family" dramatizes experiences central to the formation of a new, liberal, managerial intelligentsia, which has turned its back on the ethnic ghettos, developed a cosmopolitan outlook and cosmopolitan tastes through higher education, and now looks back on its origins with a mixture of superiority and sentimental regret. This experience, repeated now for several generations, has played a formative part in the development of the managerial and professional class. Its ideology of tolerance and anti-authoritarianism puts great emphasis on the ability to outgrow early prejudices. Because the new class has defined itself in opposition to the values of "middle America," it needs to repudiate its own roots, to exaggerate the distance it has traveled, and also to exaggerate the racism and bigotry of those lower down on the social scale. At the same time, it occasionally sheds a sentimental tear over the simpler life it thinks it has left behind.

All this finds almost classic expression in Lear's comedy of popular ignorance and parochialism. In one of the more perceptive commentaries on Lear's work, Michael J. Arlen, television critic of *The New Yorker,* suggests that "modern, psychiatrically inspired or induced ambivalence may indeed be the key dramatic principle behind this new genre of popular entertainment. A step is taken, then a step back. A gesture is made and then withdrawn—blurred into distracting laughter, or somehow forgotten."

America's new managerial elite has not only adopted an official ideology of tolerance, in which it does not yet feel completely secure, it has also developed an "anti-authoritarian" style of personal relations that forbids the expression of anger and violent emotion. "All in the Family" dissolves murderous impulses by foisting them on the father and by depicting this father, moreover, as an opinionated but impotent autocrat crushed by the wheel of historical progress. It helps the viewer not so much to come to terms with anger as to displace it. Beyond that, it reinforces the collective self-esteem of those whose ascendancy rests not on the secure command of an intellectual and political tradition but on their imagined superiority to the average unenlightened American bigot.

21.

Beyond the Pale

Mel Watkins

"In the fifties, you didn't see no part of no blacks on TV. You had to be creative if you wanted to see some brothers—had to sit there in your living room and imagine some black folks. And with the people you saw on the tube, it were not easy. I mean, yeah, there was Amos 'n' Andy and sometimes old pop-eyed Mantan Moreland in a movie running like hell from somethin' he thought he seen. But for the most part you didn't see nothin' resemblin' a spade. Me, I used to get up and turn on the radio, listen to 'The Shadow,' that's 'bout the closest thing to a spade they had on the air at the time."

This comment was overheard at a Harlem bar during a commercial break in a Saturday afternoon football broadcast, as a group of patrons bantered about how often they see blacks on television. The old-timer who made the remark—the bar's resident philosopher-comic—was, as usual, injecting a bit of irony and contention into an otherwise predictable conversation. And, as odd as they may have seemed to the younger patrons at the bar, his observations were basically correct.

Certainly, blacks' changing roles have made television-watching today a radically different experience from what it was in the early fifties, when I was a child in a small Midwestern mill town and my family purchased its first television set.

Then, any child old enough to spend Saturday afternoons at

171

the movies, to scan the newspapers occasionally, or to be aware of current radio programs, knew that for some reason—illogical as it may have been—blacks were rarely seen, heard, or mentioned anywhere in the media. When they were, they appeared in the guise of some grossly distorted burlesque figure, never more than a borderline literate—or they were perpetrators of some ghastly crime. In other words, they were *not* really blacks as I knew them. (There were very few rapists among my early acquaintances, and I just didn't know anyone for whom grinning was a constant preoccupation; media images notwithstanding, growing up in the ghetto was a very *serious* and dangerous affair.) But since no one else seemed to question the situation, I simply accepted it as just another of the strange perversions of the adult world.

Even so, my initial encounters with blacks on television during the fifties were tinged with a persistent uneasiness. I mean, to be presented with Farina, Stymie, or Buckwheat of Hal Roach's "Our Gang" comedies, with Mantan Moreland in the Charlie Chan mysteries, with Stepin Fetchit and Willie Best—and to realize that they were the *only* blacks on television—was to sense an attitude both insulting and frightening in the nonblack world beyond one's living room. *Is that the way they see me?* That question always hung there, somewhat dampening the humor of those old movies.

And if the black image in those movies (which constituted a large part of early television programming) was embarrassing, it was no better in the weekly series. One would have thought that blacks had only three occupational options: singing and dancing, working as a servant, or—again—just grinning. There was Eddie "Rochester" Anderson as a valet on Jack Benny's show, and there was Lillian Randolph as a maid on "The Great Gildersleeve." Later on, the title role in "Beulah," yet another maid's part, was played at various times by Ethel Waters, Hattie McDaniel, and Louise Waters. And of course, there was "Amos 'n' Andy." Except for entertainers such as Lena Horne, Leontyne Price, the late Nat "King" Cole, Harry Belafonte, and a few smiling faces in crowd scenes, these shows offered the only representation of blacks on early television.

Still, as sparse and distorted as that representation was, I can recall waiting anxiously in front of the television set any time a black performer was scheduled to appear. (Few blacks I knew ever missed "Amos 'n' Andy.") Despite the rapt attention, though, we rarely identified with those blacks on the home screen.

The strongest impression I derived from television in the fifties, then, was a sense of the vast distance between the black and the white worlds. Programs like "Beulah" or "The Jack Benny Show," and movies with comedians like Mantan Moreland or Stepin Fetchit, presented blacks in white environments, portraying them in such a bizarre manner that I couldn't for a second imagine they had anything to do with reality. They were about as authentic to me as Superman or Br'er Rabbit. "Amos 'n' Andy" was the only show at the time with a nearly all-black cast, and that made it a little more familiar to me. Moreover, in private—that is, not in the presence of whites—I found Kingfish's larcenous antics hilarious, and not that far-removed from those of certain people I knew who could have been his prototype. (At the time, I don't recall that any of us were aware of the more serious consequences of the burlesque images of black professionals—doctors and lawyers—perpetuated by this show.) Still, "Amos 'n' Andy" only worked to confirm my sense of the black world as an insulated, separate place from which I could only escape at considerable risk to self-esteem and safety. I have little doubt that it did the same for the fair-skinned children I saw every day in school (but never saw afterwards).

If certain social critics are right about the medium being the message, then the message of the fifties was all too clear: *"If you white, you right. If you black, get back."* Considering the grassroots idealism and optimism still alive among blacks at that time, and the visual medium's power to mold behavior patterns, the timing for those black video images was atrocious. Not only was television not suggesting even the possibility of a racially harmonious America, it was affirming just the opposite—a separatist world, where blacks were only tolerated in white society as servants, buffoons, or entertainers. It doesn't require much hindsight to recognize that the television images of the fifties and the early sixties were ruinous to black-white rapprochement. We are probably still paying for the medium's blunder with added social unrest and racial violence.

Ordinary blacks finally made their first significant television appearances during the sixties civil rights movement—not in sitcoms, but during sit-ins and on national news broadcasts. The impact was overwhelming. Suddenly, here were throngs of real, live people—until now confined by American television to the realm of the nonexistent.

For me—one of a handful of black students at a Northern college during the sixties—watching those newscasts was a shattering experience. The blatant inhumanity and brutality emerging from the confrontation between black protesters and unyielding whites brought home a hard truth: From that moment the first dog or fire-hose was turned loose on a crowd of blacks, the first black child spat upon by an enraged Southern housewife, the first skull cracked by a well-aimed nightstick, one knew that the dream of black assimilation into the fabric of American society had been set back for decades—possibly forever. For an entire generation of black children just now moving into adulthood, those were the first real images of blacks interacting with whites ever witnessed on television. They are images unlikely to be forgotten, much less forgiven.

For whites, also, this abrupt intrusion of blacks onto the television screen, and therefore into their homes, must have been appalling—whether because they empathized with the protesters and abhorred violence, or because they were hostile to those upstarts who dared step "out of their place" and threaten a monochromatic world.

The civil rights movement fizzled with minimal gains and ultimately halted under the weight of benign neglect. But it accomplished much in directing media attention to the plight of black Americans: National awareness expanded throughout the sixties with coverage of the more militant protests and race riots.

It does not seem altogether coincidental that "I Spy," the first prime-time adventure series to feature a black in a starring role, first aired in 1965, the year after race riots erupted in Philadelphia, Rochester, New York City, and Elizabeth, New Jersey, and a month after the destruction of Watts in Los Angeles. Nor is it surprising that NBC suddenly discovered an easing of resistance among advertisers and affiliated stations to the idea of a black lead in a weekly series.

And so Bill Cosby became the Jackie Robinson of network television, co-starring with Robert Culp as a CIA agent in "I Spy." Cosby, a twenty-seven-year-old nightclub comedian at the time, made his dramatic debut in the show and went on to win three successive Emmy Awards for "outstanding continued performance by an actor in a leading role in a dramatic series." Yet, despite the quality of his performances and the undeniable entertainment value of the show, I could never see the casting of Cosby as much more than a thinly disguised attempt to cool off the anger and bitterness that had ignited the Watts riot.

After all, he portrayed a character accepted by the system who continually risked his life to protect it. Moreover, at a time when the fight for equal rights had made racial violence endemic, the subject of race was seldom even touched on by Cosby or Culp. The show had absolutely nothing to do with the reality of America in 1965, and consequently had little or no effect on the growing racial tension. It did represent a breakthrough in casting, and apparently television executives thought this was enough.

But, just as early riots had spurred television networks to hire blacks both behind the scenes and on camera, continued violence in American cities—and the assassination of Martin Luther King, Jr.—intensified the drive for more adequate black representation in the television industry. Protests by black organizations about bias in the industry had also increased dramatically. In certain instances, lawsuits had been filed against television station owners and, as with WLBT in Jackson, Mississippi, some owners were threatened with loss of their federal licenses. The Federal Communications Commission had by this time adopted an antidiscrimination policy based on the 1964 Civil Rights Act.

So, with pressure from all sides, by 1968 the television industry had to give in to the push for racial balance. In typically premature fashion, network executives began to contend that "the day of equal opportunity" was near and, conceivably to prove this claim, they scheduled two new shows featuring blacks, ABC's "The Outcasts," a western starring Don Murray and Otis Young (portraying a former slave) as bounty hunters in antebellum America, and NBC's "Julia," starring Diahann Carroll.

"The Outcasts" was produced ostensibly to correct some of the flagrant distortions in "I Spy." Many of the episodes depicted conflict, even animosity, between Young and Murray, and Young's color was presented as a continuing problem for him. In other words, "The Outcasts" generally paid stricter attention than the other show to the real problems faced by blacks, but it foundered in the ratings and had a short life.

In "Julia," Diahann Carroll played the widowed mother of a six-year-old child. The first television series to focus on a black family, "Julia" conspicuously lacked a father figure. But the harsh criticism the show received still seemed undeserved. While Julia and her son Corry were not typical blacks, they weren't inconceivable. They did not reflect the attitudes or mores of the black masses, but they were representative of black middle-class attitudes, which (like Julia herself) were extremely light if not quite white. But then, that was the rub.

Black, for many critics in the late sixties, meant *distinctively* black. That was associated only with the black lower classes, who were, and still are, the prime victims of American racism. "Julia" had little to do with them. Diahann Carroll herself described the show as "lightweight entertainment that was about as true to life as any other series." Still, no judgment of the show seemed more apt at the time than a friend of mine's remark, "Julia fiddles while Chicago burns."

Not until the late sixties, when militancy had become the dominant mood among blacks and the battle had literally been taken to the streets, did the television industry fully respond. And even then, its only offerings generally ignored the crisis of black-white conflict. There were exceptions, of course, such as the CBS "Black America" documentary series, which began with the Bill Cosby-narrated "Black History: Lost, Stolen, or Strayed." Ironically, that segment spent considerable time pointing out the distorted images of blacks that Hollywood had introduced and television had perpetuated—lazy, shiftless darkies, cowardly buffoons, lecherous ne'er-do-wells. The 1968 television season may have eliminated insulting portraits of blacks, but it left me with as much uneasiness as had the past distortions.

That season did at least mark the beginning of an era, however. Blacks no longer had to fight merely to appear. For nearly a decade, practically every show had a black actor or actress in a continuing role, or frequently included a black performer in one of its episodes. Variety shows usually had one or more black guests, although few blacks hosted such programs. The public pressure of the late sixties and the lagging economy of the seventies drove sponsors to seek out "special markets," so blacks began appearing regularly in commercials as well.

The number of blacks on the air reached a peak during the seventies, when several shows with nearly all-black casts ("Good Times"; "The Jeffersons"; the original "Sanford and Son"; "What's Happening!!") were aired. Only "The Jeffersons" has lasted. The others have been replaced by programs featuring black performers in integrated casts. And these shows have run the gamut: from "Diff'rent Strokes," starring Gary Coleman as a precocious child living with his adoptive white family, to "Sanford," with Redd Foxx as the grizzled, acerbic junk dealer playing opposite a nonblack employee. Although blacks remain plainly visible during television's peak hours, the number of blacks in regular roles on weekly, prime-time network shows has noticeably diminished in the past few years.

Moreover, as a recent Civil Rights Commission report stated, blacks appearing on television are disproportionately cast as teenagers and in situation comedies. Since 1968, almost all new weekly series starring blacks fit into one of these categories. Only the short-lived "Bill Cosby Show," in which Cosby portrayed a schoolteacher and coach, even attempted any serious depiction of black life.

There have so far been no long-lasting dramatic series (to compare with "The Waltons," "Lou Grant," or even "Little House on the Prairie") focusing on black life in America—except for "Harris and Company," which aired only briefly in 1979, and "Palmerstown, USA," the Norman Lear-Alex Haley production shelved after an inauspicious beginning. And the few dramatic specials seen on network television, with the exception of "Roots" and "Roots II," have drawn severe criticism from blacks. In 1980 an organization was formed specifically to prevent the airing of the NBC television drama "Beulah Land." In this instance the film's title was indicative of its content, and the black organization protested the "offensive and degrading stereotypes that perpetuate the image of the slave as ignorant, oversexed, slovenly, dependent on the whim of his master, and filled with love for that master and the master's land." Some minor changes were made in the script of "Beulah Land," although the producer contends they were not in response to the protests. The film eventually ran, and critics justifiably pointed out that the grossness of its stereotypes was matched only by the inanity of its plot.

Commercial television's staple program form—especially for its black performers—is not the serious drama. It is the situation comedy, which requires extreme oversimplification in its quest for humor, and practically prohibits any exploration of contemporary life. These limitations notwithstanding, two black sitcom characters—George Jefferson and Fred Sanford—have occasionally provided accurate glimpses of black attitudes.

As Jefferson, Sherman Hemsley portrays a black man who, after building a thriving laundry business, has moved his family into a luxurious Upper East Side apartment in New York City. Jefferson is an odd combination of the aggressive, materialistic, successful businessman and the pompously proud black man. He is as anti-white as Archie Bunker is anti-black, and just as Bunker's gibes about minorities are defused by his prevailing ineptitude and stubborn self-righteousness, Jefferson's insistently caustic racial remarks are made acceptable by his ultimate buffoonery. Still, humor is often double-edged; just as there is a considerable segment of the nonblack television audience sharing Bunker's attitudes toward minorities, Jefferson's cynicism about whites and most American ideals (excluding the pursuit of money) reflects the sentiments of many blacks.

Similarly, Redd Foxx's portrayal of Sanford, despite the comic guise, often provides insight into a skepticism of middle-class values common among blacks. Sanford's stubborn insistence on maintaining his own identity reflects a genuine black attitude. And he also mirrors the shift in black perspective over the recent decades—from a self-conscious denial of so-called black behavior to an assertive flaunting of it.

In both "The Jeffersons" and "Sanford," however, the performers themselves are responsible for conveying this real-life quality. They must go beyond the script to do so. Neither show clearly expresses the style of humor traditional to black communities.

It is distressing for one who grew up with that distinctive black style of humor on street corners, and later in theaters like the Apollo, to miss it in most television sitcoms—even in those with black comedians. This conspicuous lack speaks of the networks' blinkered devotion to the wants of the majority. According to some blacks inside the industry, the absence of the black style of humor may be a prime reason for the gradual disappearance of black shows on television.

According to Matt Robinson, a black writer and producer whose credits include the films *Save the Children* and *Amazing Grace,* "all comedy on television is based on the Jewish comedy style—the style of the borscht-belt standup comedians who do gags with a rapid-fire approach: setup-setup-punch line. The style was adopted because it solved the technical problem of television's having to get everything in quickly. Because it is a fast medium, you have to grab the audience quickly, within the first thirty seconds or so, or else they change the channel.

"In a show like 'Sanford,' for instance, the tone of the humor is often black, the material is black-oriented, but the structure follows the same formula as any other television show. It's based on the unlikely proposition, as we all know, that there is always someone standing around with witty, flippant responses for anything that's said. That's not a black development.

"I think black humor stopped being a dominant force with the advent of television. Black humor, to me, is that stage-show type of humor that flowed from specific characters and situations that were familiar to other blacks—almost exclusively so."

Many white writers agree with Robinson's assessment of television humor. According to Dick Baer, who has written scripts for black sitcoms like "What's Happening!!" and who now writes for "Archie Bunker's Place," "Comedy dealing with racial matters has to do with what people expect blacks to do. To a certain extent, it's what blacks expect blacks to do. But since whites are in the majority, they make the decisions about how blacks are going to figure into the entertainment industry. They are working both sides of the streets. They are selling non-servile blacks to placate the black audience and at the same time showing stupid or amoral blacks or unrealistic blacks to satisfy the white audiences' assumptions about blacks."

Bob Peete, a black writer who worked on "The Bill Cosby Show" and was a story editor for "Good Times," explains it another way: "There is a real difference between black and white humor. The chief distinction is that black humor is more attitudinal; it's not what you say, but how you say it. The attitude imported to the line gets the laugh. For instance, if Redd Foxx is on camera and someone knocks at the door, Redd might say, 'Come in,' and the audience would crack up. Now 'come in' is obviously not a joke, but with Redd it can be funny. Richard Pryor does the same thing, he doesn't tell jokes. On the other hand, white humor is structured to a straight-line-punch-line format."

According to some black performers and writers, the disparity between creation and performance in a black sitcom adversely affects the quality of the material, which in turn almost assures the show's failure. "It's a self-fulfilling type situation," comments one writer. "White writers produce mediocre shows about blacks and, when they fail, decide that the audience doesn't want black shows. Therefore, fewer shows are produced."

The reasons for the dwindling number of black shows on television may or may not be that simple. It is clear, however, that television sitcoms are a virtual wasteland when it comes to authentic black humor—despite the work of Redd Foxx, Sherman Hemsley, Robert Guillaume, and Ja'net DuBois (of the defunct "Good Times"). Some black comedians, such as Richard

Pryor, have refused to attempt molding their humor into the sitcom format. Since blacks are predominantly represented on television in sitcoms, a more authentic prime-time view of black style and attitudes seems extremely bleak.

One possible remedy for the situation has been suggested by comic actor Cleavon Little: "I've been doing pilots for years and they've failed, I think, because they've all had white writers, white producers, and white directors. If we had blacks doing those things—all of them—we could bring another kind of ethos, nuance, to the comedy. That hasn't been investigated. Let us try, control our own humor, and I'm sure you'd see a difference."

No network has yet agreed to this proposal. But, if the present trend continues on network television, the problem for many black viewers seeking more realistic reflection of their own culture during prime time may again become as it was for that Harlem bar's resident sage—a matter of imagination.

22.

One Man's Soap

William H. Pritchard

Several years ago I suffered what I feared would be an irreparable loss; not of the tragic sort—the death of a loved one or the grievous ending to some human relationship—but of a sort curiously painful nonetheless. "Somerset," a soap opera I had become deeply devoted to, ended its run; and on December 31, 1976—in a shocking half-hour of reconciliations, tying up loose ends (not all of them got tied up), and generally empty affirmations—the show disappeared forever. It would have been a sensible time for me to form a New Year's resolution and decide to spend that half-hour after lunch engaged in some admirable pursuit like reading through Gibbon's *Decline and Fall of the Roman Empire,* or buying a pair of running shoes, some funny clothes, and preparing to run a bit up and down my local Northampton Road. Oddly enough these alternatives never entered my head. After a few days of mourning, and of surly midday dissatisfactions, I sat down for a serious session with *TV Guide* by way of mapping out a strategy for latching onto a new Soap.

Although for the leisured housewife or lazy college student, many Soap-viewing possibilities exist, the rigidity of my own habits precluded much freedom in choosing. The Soap had to occur in the 12:30-1:30 time period and had to be of the half-hour variety—a whole hour of watching takes too large a chunk out of the day in which books have to be read. For a time I tried "Lovers and Friends," a charmless, short-lived replacement for "Somerset," then I watched a bit of "The Young and the Restless," but found it filled with too many beautiful young people talking to excess about their various "hangups" and how so-and-so had "copped out" or been "hassled" in some manner or other, usually sexual. Clearly "The Young and the Restless" would not do for a man of settled habits, even though it dealt with controversial matters like birth control pills. "Ryan's Hope" had been highly praised for its vigorous characterizations and on-site photography, but it was an Irish soap, filled with wonderful lovable Irish characters—not the sort of thing for a Welshman of morose leanings.

That left "Search for Tommorrow," a half-hour show which I was delighted to find out had premiered in 1951, thus making it, along with "Love of Life" (since deceased), the most venerable of all the soaps. By that spring I had settled into becoming a "Search"-watcher, and now consider myself an authoritative commentator on the whole affair. Let me therefore tell you a bit about the characters and their situations, and then try to explain how someone in his right mind (my current illusion about myself) could become enthralled with the whole operation for years on end.

To begin with, there is the amorphous, elusive title. "Somerset" was the straightforward name of a small town in Michigan where things took place, but "Search for Tomorrow"? Whose search, and just how "for tomorrow"? Clearly an old-fashioned radio soap opera title, like "Life Can Be Beautiful" or "The Guiding Light" (the latter now on television), meant to evoke romantic yearnings and a vaguely uplifted sense that there's Something More To It All than there appears to be day by day. It would have been too simple, I guess, to title the show "Henderson," the imaginary town where its action takes place. Henderson is out there somewhere in the Midwest, southern Illinois maybe. There are oil fields to the south, and people often have to fly down to New Orleans, home of the powerful Sentell family, a number of whose members have moved to Henderson for obvious reasons of plot.

Henderson has, of course, a hospital, in fact two hospitals (one on the "other side of town"), into which various members of the cast are taken or wheeled for attention to their assorted brands of blindness, leukemia, slight skull fractures, or brain tumors pressing on the optic nerve causing major headaches. They will be cared for there, in Henderson Hospital, by Dr. Bob Rogers, head of it all, good friends with most of the cast (he's seen 'em come and go), and filled with the richest bedside manner.

When people are not in the hospital they tend to gather at the Hartford House or Inn, run by the two oldest members—from point of service—of the "Search" cast, Joanne (Jo) Tourneur (for years Jo Vincent, but recently married yet once more) and "Stu" Bergmann. Jo (played by Mary Stuart, who has been with the show since its inception and is thus accorded star status) is, quite simply, the finest person in the world. Not an ounce of pretentiousness, or greed, or envy, or lust (that I can detect) or pettiness or rancor or any other of the deadly and not-so-deadly sins stains this lady's character. A fount of homely wisdom with a wonderful temperament, Jo has lived all her life in Henderson; indeed she behaved in New Orleans, when she visited there recently, as if it were as morally remote as Tangier. Stu, co-owner of the inn and married to Ellie—a woman whose simplicity makes Jo look sophisticated—is, as he would like to say about himself and often does, a man of relatively few words and basic human decency. He will take a drink, but only now and then, and if he has more than one becomes wholly confused and infantile, then winds up being put to bed by Ellie and catching a bad cold as a result of his folly.

Though Stu is simple, he knows what he likes (and it's not Art). Or rather what he doesn't like. He doesn't like charming, verbally articulate men who attempt and succeed in winning the affections of (1) Jo, or (2) his daughter, Janet Collins, who is especially prone to disastrous affairs of the heart. He would be equally enraged if one of these men tried to cotton up to (3) Janet's daughter, Liza, or (4) Ellie. Fortunately for Stu, Liza is completely wrapped up in her dashingly handsome, extraordinarily rich and powerful husband, Travis Tourneur ("Rusty") Sentell, and their recently adopted baby. While nobody has ever been seen making a play for Ellie.

Anyone who watches "Search" for a while becomes aware of certain patterns, which by their repetition provide an odd satisfaction. Let me run through a few of these, by subject:

Books. Nobody is ever caught dead reading a book, unless he or she (most probably she) is in a blue funk about her love life. If she is interrupted while reading a book (and it will never be named, just referred to as "a book," not the *Aeneid* or *Shōgun*), she will gratefully put it down and launch into an explanation, to the interruptor, of "what's wrong." More likely she will be leafing through a magazine in the most idle manner, just looking to begin the next conversation about Problems. (Of course, it would be hard to make an exciting scene out of someone reading the *Aeneid,* or even *Shōgun.)* At times (at least on "Search") poetry is quoted, usually Shakespeare, often inaccurately or with lines left out so as to make it more "understandable." Shakespeare by the way—especially *Romeo and Juliet*—is Wonderful, even though no sane person would be found reading him.

Food. People are often seen dining, either at the Hartford House or at Ernesto's (one of those terrific little Italian restaurants everybody loves), but there is never a visible piece of food disappearing into anyone's chops. Usually people toy with their food ("You're hardly eating anything"), find that they're "not hungry," and launch once more into talk about Problems. Women tend to eat something like a spinach salad for lunch, never (say) corned beef and cabbage or Yankee Pot Roast (perhaps unavailable in Henderson). They are tempted by the dessert, but abstain because of the calorie count. Men are inclined to eat more meat.

Drink. Stephanie Wyatt, the closest thing to a "bad" woman on the Soap, is allowed to have a martini, which she does quite often. Other women, if they indulge at all, will invariably have a glass of white wine (what, by the way, is wrong with red wine?) but never seem to drink it. Whiskey in private houses is always there in a decanter; never is a bottle visible. Younger, poorer types have been known to have a beer. Everybody drinks coffee, endlessly, all the time, all characters evidently possessing cast-iron stomachs. Nobody asks for Sanka instead. Diet soda is a possibility; also champagne on festive occasions.

Sex. Perhaps I should have put this earlier, but there is relatively little sex on "Search," though heterosexual relationships are the staple of the show (no homosexuals that I've noticed). Lovemaking is highly romanticized, bodies and faces blur and swirl so you can't make out what's going on and of course nothing really is. "Haunting" melodies fill the air. There is occasionally some intense kissing that is not much fun to watch. Some characters are allowed dream-fantasies in which they meet their partner all dressed up in beautiful clothes, at some fancy occasion. The heroic male really does Sweep the Heroine Off Her Feet, something that is often difficult to accomplish in real life (I speak from personal experience). In very serious scenes preparatory to lovemaking, we get a glimpse of the male's naked torso. This must be fairly well covered with hair, at least it seems to be *de rigueur* for a job on "Search." There is little extramarital sex—not much at all in the way of "illicit" goings-on. We must remember that this show has been running for thirty years and has its roots in the sensible pieties of the fifties. Sometimes the dialogue becomes forcefully explicit, as when Stephanie, speaking of the perils her eighteen-year-old daughter Wendy is exposed to, opines that young people of that age like to get to know each other well—"and I *do* mean in bed," she adds, with one of her fine wisdom-of-experience facial expressions. Or there was the following exchange when lawyer Kathy Phillips tried to compliment Garth the Artist (he is a *very* difficult, unconventional fellow) on his dealings with her young son, Doug. Kathy: "You're very good with little boys." Garth: "I'm not so bad with big girls either." You see the force of that innuendo.

Religion. Almost everybody believes in Something, but nobody has any words for it. People don't go to church except for the occasional funeral or wedding. Catholic, Protestant, Jew—it's all the same, presumably.

Race. There is an occasional black, often an assistant lieutenant in the police department who works for a slower-witted white man (the black is invariably clever). But nonwhites appear only intermittently and are never given quite enough to do.

Children. Invariably blond-headed, incredibly cute, good at putting their arms around their (divorced) mother and saying how much they love her, which brings tears to her lonely eyes. Infants, of course, are always a good investment of time.

The Aged. Not usually visible on "Search," though at the moment a whole series of credulous oldsters have gone to Jamaica with evil Dr. Winston Kyle to be (don't they wish) cured of their afflictions by his faith-healing.

Pot. Nobody on "Search" smokes pot, thank God.

Jogging or Running. Nobody on "Search" jogs or runs, except in pursuit of someone. I don't quite understand the absence of this practice but don't really object to it either.

Christmas is a good time to watch "Search" because it shows off, by contrast, one's own real life Scrooge-like tendencies. "I love Christmas, I love to wrap presents," breathes Jo, a light in her eyes, many wrapped presents testifying to this enthusiasm. But we know it can't go on for long, that happiness, and indeed within minutes Martin's playing of the market has become an issue, has caused the light in Jo's eyes to be replaced by the pained, martyred forbearance she is so good at expressing. In the midst of Christmas joy, trouble lies ahead.

But of course in the Soap, as in life, trouble always lies ahead, the difference being that the hooked viewer feeds on this trouble and finds it exhilarating, both in anticipation and in the event. I know someone who avoids depressing movies because she says there's enough sadness in life. The viewer of a soap would like to avoid, or postpone considering until evening, the sadness and trouble lying about him in the world outside, and ahead in his own life—so he cultivates its daily occurrence on the television screen. At least my life is not, for the moment, as hopeless as *that* one, says he. At least (looking at despondent Lee Sentell, staring gloomily at a beautifully decorated Christmas tree) *my* fiancée does not have a brain tumor and has not been spirited away by Dr. Kyle to Jamaica, there to be subject to his "incredible power over women, *in every way*" (as Lee has been informed). But then, a paper Santa Claus hung on the tree miraculously turns into the fiancée, Sunny Adamson, who says to her Lee, "Hello there, Gloomy-Face," and proceeds to remove her Santa Claus cap and cloak! They embrace fiercely, until the vision fades.

From the tone of this report it may seem to you that my interest in "Search" consists wholly in picking apart its absurdities, unrealities, and generally half-baked attitudes, which I as a superior person don't share. I think you would, however, be wrong. How superior can one be toward an event that provides one daily sustenance? On the other hand, there has of late been a compensatory inflation in the value of Soaps—claims made that here is where the finest acting anywhere is to be found, or where certain social, cultural, medical facts are at least recognized. Though the acting is good enough for my tastes, and though I suppose you could say that an issue (like alternatives to surgery) is at least raised, I can't believe that therein lies the Soap's real power to compel. Its compellingness has more to do with the construction of a world—not a world of complex thought or psychological penetration, but a world nonetheless—full of names, faces, voices, gestures, and attitudes that impress themselves on our ears and eyes and that don't disappear after a half-hour or hour as they do on evening television. Or rather, we *know* that they will be back tomorrow, certainly the next day; that five days a week, give or take an occasional national holiday they will be there for us on CBS.

It is the ongoingness of "Search," or of any Soap, that is the key to its power and that a person untouched by this power can never understand. How many times have I heard someone say authoritatively about a Soap that "nothing ever happens in them. I watched one for a while, missed three weeks of it, turned it back on and they were still talking about the same things" —as if that settled it for the Soap. I may ask in return, "What do you want to happen on the shows you watch?" Try "Vega$" or "Starsky and Hutch" if you like a snappy little incident begun, middled, and ended over the course of an hour. Something happens in our life every day; at least we grow older, finish one thing, begin another, lose this and gain that. But "Search," though certain characters come and eventually go, remains essentially the same. Time stretches out endlessly, it seems, for the latest complication is clearly going to take months until it begins, even slightly, to unravel. And as it just goes along, nothing really happening, one suddenly finds oneself pleased or moved by the merest, smallest thing—a gesture, a twist of the voice, a way of saying something. (David Sutton, an admirable character, has a way of saying "Thank you," sincerely, that makes me feel life is worth living.) You never quite know at what moment something strangely evocative may occur, but you can only respond to these moments if you've sat around many months or years and watched programs that evoke nothing.

A few final remarks: The most painful moment for any Soap watcher is when a visitor or guest says, "Please go ahead and watch your program . . . what is it . . . "Reach For the Sky?" maybe I'll watch it with you." In any event, total silence must be enforced, else you may be confronted with questions like "Who is she?" or "What is that?" which reduce the hardened viewer to stuttering confusion and despair. How can this outsider ever begin to understand what is so deep within your bones? Also, if you are going to watch "Search" you must plan to be unavailable for any business or friendly lunches, brown-bag, intimate, or otherwise. When colleagues (I am a teacher) suggest that our department might meet next Tuesday at noon or 12:30, I find myself devising various stratagems by which to disentangle myself—but how many dental appointments can one legit-imately claim to have? Conferences with students must be ended briskly with the phrase, mumbled in some haste, "I have an appointment with . . ." (the rest left indistinct). Once I quitted a friend under the pretense of having to see a person named Somer-set. I suppose he could as well have been named Search. And since I dislike taking the phone off the hook, there is always the chance that it will ring (who could be calling at this hour?), in which case the thing to do is to say quite urgently and intensely, "Can I call you back in fifteen, (twenty, ten) minutes?" then rush back into the inside world.

There are some lines from a poem by David Slavitt that say as well as anything I know what is involved in watching a Soap. Mr. Slavitt's favorite appears to be "All My Children," but the name hardly matters, as he lays out the essence of them all:

> They wade through sorrows scriptwriters devise
> in kitchens, hospital rooms, divorce courts, jails
> or cemeteries, and nearly everyone tries
> to do the right thing. And everyone fails.

Slavitt goes on to note the usually "desperate" mood of these characters whose "happiness is only a setup for woe," then concludes with the following confession:

> Stupid, I used to think, and partly still
> do, deploring the style, the mawkishness.
> And yet, I watch. I cannot get my fill
> of lives as dumb as mine: Pine Valley's mess
> is comforting. I need not wish them ill.
> I watch, and I delight in, their distress.

That "delight" may not be the Eternal Delight that William Blake once identified with Energy, but in a world of time, not Eternity, it does pretty well.

23.

And Gracie Begat Lucy Who Begat Laverne

Michael Malone

By changing fashions to fit the times, by loosening their themes and tightening their T-shirts, a few daytime television epics of domestic calamity have somehow managed to defy age and to live on all the days of our lives; indeed, of our parents' lives and perhaps our children's as well. No prime-time series, however, has ever proved so impervious to shifting seasons. Even the most successful appear to have a natural life span, to grow old and lose their ratings, to be left for younger rivals.

But inevitably, when this love affair between the American public and some popular television series comes to an end, its absence leaves behind, unsatisfied, whatever fantasy or emotional need that particular departed show had been managing to fulfill in our culture. Inevitably, a new program is born to replace the old: We lose Lucy and Ethel but we gain their daughters, Laverne and Shirley. Ozzie and Harriet may have departed but, safe in the "Happy Days" of the fifties, Richie's family is as good and wise as Ricky Nelson's once was. And if Ricky's singing could transform a family show into a vehicle for a teenage idol, so twenty years later, in a program planned around Richie's family, could Henry Winkler's Fonz skyrocket into a preteen merchandizing industry. In some ways, Archie Bunker's father is Ralph Kramden and his grandfather Chester A. Riley. "All in the Family" belongs to a family.

These parental predecessors can be traced back along the branches of television's family tree. And it is in this genealogy of popular series that the heart of the medium can be found: The most persistent (and therefore presumably the most meaningful) themes and relationships of our favorite shows—the situation comedies—tell us who we think we are, or want to be. (In a talk on film criticism Pauline Kael gave at Harvard in the early seventies, she earnestly urged budding movie analysts to take up television study instead, because of its incomprehensibly vast and almost entirely unexplored influence, more pervasive than any force since the medieval church.) Again and again, the same esssential features appear, not merely because producers are consciously trying to reassemble the ingredients of earlier successes, but because they are unconsciously resupplying those collective myths and types of characters intrinsic to the genre and important to our culture.

The show ubiquitously known as the "sitcom" has outlasted or outdrawn our fifties craze for thirty-nine cowboy shows a week, our sixties craze for doctors and lawyers, and even our perennial infatuation with idiosyncratic detectives like blind Longstreet, crippled Ironside, bumbling Columbo, obese Cannon, and bald, dapper Kojak. The sitcom has trounced in ratings and durability satiric comedy styles of the British "Monty Python" sort, or of the "spoof" series— "Get Smart" and "Batman" —and every other type of television show. Today, situation comedies regularly number three out of the four top-rated prime-time programs. They are thirty-minute shows with descendants going back thirty years.

That this is the favorite format should not surprise us; it is preeminently suited to the medium of television entertainment, for technical as well as social reasons. A television screen is a small opening in a box, very like the little proscenium of a puppet theater. Seated in the familiar surroundings of our homes, we are watching four-inch-high people scurrying across this opening. In sitcoms they are usually getting themselves caught up in mistakes, misunderstandings, or mishaps; their actions get faster and broadly physical, they shout and pout and then kiss and patch up. It is all very much like a Punch-and-Judy show. Television cannot sustain the epic or the tragic stance, which asks for very different aesthetic and psychological responses: For one thing, such drama demands that we see characters as greater than ourselves, which is difficult to do when they are only four inches high and in our own ordinary living rooms. Nor can television evoke, as films can, the awed wonder of romance. The mythic stature accorded deified images like Gable or Garbo on a *literally* larger-than-life screen, viewed in the vast dark communal space of a movie theater, is laughably incongruous if transferred to television.

By its nature, television lends itself not to tragedy and myth but to comedy and domesticity, the foundation of situation comedy. (They are also the foundation of commercials, a form indigenous to television and a close relative of the sitcom.) All comedy is domestic in the sense that its harmonizing function moves it toward marriage, family, and community, and away from the great solitude of heroics and grand romance. But the particular kind of domesticity celebrated in situation comedies is the significant result of television having come into its own during the early fifties, when family values reigned supreme in America. Then the virtues of the self-contained and happy suburban home governed our culture in ways that had not been true before and are unlikely to recur in our own cynical times. The early comedies like "Ozzie and Harriet" symbolized domestic utopia: every family in its own private home, every home with a television set for each member. The medium, like the suburban mode of life, fostered uniformity but not community. From their middle-class living rooms, monogamous couples and their happy, wholesome children stared into the middle-class living rooms of the Nelsons or the Erwins ("The Trouble with Father") or the Andersons ("Father Knows Best") or the Williamses ("Make Room for Daddy") or the Ricardos ("I Love Lucy"), and saw themselves affably mirrored there. Of course, the pushing problem of "making it" never got its foot in the door of early sitcoms. What did Ozzie Nelson do for a living, anyhow?

As commonly used, "situation comedy" means any continuing series of half-hour comic episodes in which members of a regular cast get involved in an amusingly troublesome incident; quick complications entangle them, and an even quicker resolution unravels everything.

Among the many reasons for the sitcom's becoming television's typical programming style was that its half-hour length was perfect for a continuing series. Not only were audiences comfortable with this format from radio days, but back in the time when a show was fully sponsored by a single company, most advertisers were reluctant to double their expenses—and their risk of failure—by taking on an hour-long program.

Some critics, among them Horace Newcomb in *TV: The Most Popular Art,* want to separate *situation* comedies like "I Love Lucy" (with its physical farce, fixed characters, and emphasis on plot rather than interaction), from *domestic* comedies like "My Three Sons" (with its gentler humor, developing characters, and emphasis on human relationships). And it is true that only the loosest definition of sitcom could cover at once the slapstick cartoon buffoonery of "The Misadventures of Sheriff Lobo," the social satire of "M*A*S*H," and the warm-hearted sermonizing of "The Brady Bunch." In fact, new labels such as "dramedy" and "com-dram" have recently been dreamed up for such programs as "Eight Is Enough," which are only comedies in the sense that they espouse the "happy ending," not in the sense that they have the "witty" dialogue, incongruities, and absurd coincidences of laugh-producing plots. Brandy French, manager of program development for Columbia Pictures Television Syndication, describes such Garry Marshall series as "Happy Days" and "Laverne & Shirley" as "dramalettes," a hybrid of the orthodox sitcom and the instructional moral fable popular in the fifties. Significantly, both these shows are *set* in the fifties, and in both we can see how the distinctions between sitcom and domestic comedy blur.

Both "Laverne & Shirley" and its parent "Lucy" have fixed characters (two women, two men), fixed realistic sets, and a weekly problem that builds to some slap-stick climax. One incident (the famous mayhem in a production-line skit) offers a typical example: Working in a candy factory, Lucy and Ethel fall hopelessly behind when the conveyor belt speeds up. Physical chaos is the result. Opening a restaurant by themselves, Laverne and Shirley fall hopelessly behind, as cook and waitress, when the orders speed up. Physical chaos is the comic result. Lucy and Ethel try to break into show business. Laverne and Shirley try to break into modeling. But unlike the absolutely ritualized chicaneries, calamities, and ultimate remorse into which Lucy fell—her tearful bawling was always laughable—Laverne's and Shirley's hurts and humiliations are more apt to be treated "seriously," so that we are asked to respond first with sympathetic sentiment; then comes the joke, and we're released into laughter.

Television comedy's family tree has three major branches coming from the actual root of all drama—human relationships. They might be called *tribal* comedy, *family* comedy, and *couple* comedy. Beginning with its parent series, "You'll Never Get Rich"

("The Phil Silvers Show"), tribal comedy brings together, often around a central star, a diverse assortment of characters whose separate lives are connected by some external situation—usually the workplace (as in "The Mary Tyler Moore Show," "Alice," "Barney Miller," "Taxi," or "WKRP in Cincinnati"), but sometimes war (as in Sergeant Bilko's offspring, "McHale's Navy," or "Hogan's Heroes," or "M*A*S*H"). The student tribes beleaguering our Miss Brooks and Mr. Kotter provide a variation on the work-colleague show. Surviving a shipwreck—the excuse for "Gilligan's Island" —is, like war, an extraordinary circumstance forcing together strange bedfellows.

Initially the casts of these tribal series are apt to be ensembles of stock characters: an egghead, a dreamer, a Don Juan, a cynic, an innocent. Many series include some version of (or parodic inversion of) the sexpot/dumb-blonde female, one of our most venerable comic types, with an ancestral line reaching back through the likes of Suzanne Somers to Goldie Hawn to Marilyn Monroe to Jean Harlow. Tina Louise in "Gilligan's Island" was pretty much the pure stereotype. "WKRP in Cincinnati" turns the cliché around. There, Jennifer, played by Loni Anderson, looks like a classic dumb-blonde bombshell but proves to be an intelligent woman with a strong sense of irony. In "M*A*S*H," Loretta Swit's character is neither a ding-bat nor a sexual joke, despite her name, "Hot Lips." "The Mary Tyler Moore Show" gave us, in Georgette and Phyllis, two different portraits of a dumb blonde (sans sex), each inimitable. Indeed, if a series has good writers and good actors, and the luck of longevity, all its characters will grow in substance until we can no longer even remember the form in which we first knew them.

The group is ostensibly a random collection of adult strangers, but is subliminally an extended family ("the 'Taxi' family") with authoritative or permissive parent surrogates and older or younger siblings. Barney Miller is a good "father." Ted Baxter was the bad baby of "The Mary Tyler Moore Show." And as in real families, members may grow up and move away; this rite of passage is called the spinoff. From the Moore show alone came "Rhoda," "Phyllis," and "Lou Grant." But it is rare for a spinoff to do as well as a parent show. Brandy French suggests that the spinoff dilutes the very *community* developed by the original ensemble, the "family" togetherness that brought success.

A few shows, like the Dick Van Dyke and Bob Newhart series, bridge the tribal and familial formats, intermixing home and work life, though true *family* comedies spend more time where the bread is baked than where it is won. In the beginning, family comedies generally came equipped with both parents, and the male got star billing. All children were highly visible (not merely title characters like "Leave It to Beaver" or "Dennis the Menace"); their troubles or trouble-making frequently provided the story line. After all, in the fifties, successfully raising children in the upwardly mobile family was supposed to be the goal.

The first family series can be divided into two types: There was the "wise dad" style of "Father Knows Best," in which father, with a little help from loyal, practical mom, quietly guided the family from one *right* solution to another. "Make Room for Daddy," "The Jimmy Stewart Show," "The Brady Bunch," and "Eight Is Enough" are all, in different ways, sage sons of "Father Knows Best." At the same time we had the "dumb dad" style— the inversion of this fifties ideal. There was "The Trouble with Father," in which Stu Erwin needed a lot of help from his loving, wise wife and tolerant daughters. Chester A. Riley of "The Life of Riley" was even more a blundering victim of endless mishaps; in fact, old Rile was an idiot—like his relatives, Ralph Kramden, Fred Flintstone, and Archie Bunker—without even a modicum of internal awareness.

As the fifties glided into the sixties, family sitcoms began to reflect the cracks in the mirror of our domestic bliss. As if designed to show the dream to be a nightmare, "The Addams Family" and "The Munsters" gave us comedies about two perfectly nice, happy, harmonious middle-class families, who are completely unaware that they *horrify* because they are inhuman monsters. Urbanites go to "Green Acres," where they are ridiculously out of place. "The Beverly Hillbillies" naively insist on their old-time mountain ways in the midst of modern Los Angeles, where the Clampetts (all very nice people) make no sense to anyone.

In one new series after another, the family unit was broken and one parent disappeared. It was usually the mother, as if the wives of the fifties had already heard the distant trumpet of the women's movement and had charged away, leaving the bread in the toaster. Wise dad (or wise uncle or wise guardian) was left to carry on alone. He did just fine without a wife; in fact, without the distractions of a spouse he made a marvelously attentive parent. Who could ask for more words of wisdom than Fred MacMurray gave his boys on "My Three Sons"? Though not necessary, a surrogate mother was nice, like Aunt Bea on "The Andy Griffith Show" or Mrs. Livingston on "The Courtship of Eddie's Father." But it didn't need to be a female; for example, Mr. French the butler played the role in "Family Affair," as did Uncle Charley in "My Three Sons."

While single-father series continue to be made ("Diff'rent Strokes"), they have been superceded in popularity since the late emancipating sixties by the single-mother series, one of the first of which dealt with the trials and triumphs of a black widow with a small son. "Julia" had to work as a nurse; the mother of "The Partridge Family" smartly turned her large brood into a well-paying rock group. Other mothers sought help where they could find it: Mrs. Muir found a father-figure for her children (albeit an insubstantial one) in a virile, seafaring ghost. In current comedies like "Alice" and "One Day at a Time," single female parents tend to have deeper problems, stronger needs, and more realistic lives. Mel's bustling diner is worlds away from the quiet tree-shady house where father knew best. Alice doesn't live there anymore.

The third kind of situation comedy, structured around a *couple,* is the most popular of all. Ever since Lucy Ricardo first sent Ricky into a Spanish sputter, and crafty Kingfish first outfoxed gullible Andy, the odd-couple relationship has lain at the core of successful television comedies, as indeed it lies at the core of many great comic novels. Don Quixote and Candide tumble unscathed and unaware through the threatening chaos they have wandered into, or helped create, as their more sensible partners try to save them. In sitcoms the kooks are often the wives, and the pragmatic straightmen their exasperated husbands—as in "I Love Lucy", "I Married Joan," Burns and Allen (with the unforgettable Gracie's inspired non sequiturs), and "All in the Family." But the duo may be daughter and father ("My Little Margie"), or son and father ("Sanford and Son").

By personality traits or living habits, these two people are profoundly incompatible; one is compulsive, the other a slob; one is an ideologue, the other apolitical. The comedy in "The Odd Couple," "Maude," and "Angie" stems from such mis-matches. A few sitcoms have taken the eccentricity of the zany partner to its logical extreme by creating a character who is literally fantastical. In "Bewitched" and "I Dream of Jeannie," we meet two stereotypes of the middle-class male, each with an all-American career—one's an advertising executive, the other an astronaut. Both have the comic misfortune to love and be loved by a gorgeous woman with supernatural powers. Samantha of "Bewitched" is a witch; Jeannie is a genie. Their magic is so vast that they could give these men whatever their hearts desired. The comedy erupts when the men try forcing the women to be ordinary middle-class wives, and not to use their scary powers even for so much as defrosting ground chuck.

"Mork & Mindy" charmingly turns this stereotype on its head by making the male the kooky extraterrestrial and Mindy his down-to-earth straight-human. In fact, compared to the Orkan Mork, Lucy is no sillier than Eric Sevareid. Also in "Mork & Mindy," we recover a little bit of the sexual and romantic love that has been intrinsic to comedy since its classical origins (boy gets girl) but has never been much in evidence in sitcoms—again because of their birth in the fifties. Mork's oddness makes it possible for him to live with Mindy while keeping their relationship safe in that suspended eroticism that heightens romance and honors the censors at the same time. For all its risqué double-entendres, "Three's Company" (reflecting the new "swinging life styles" —two women and a man) depends on the same "will they or won't they?" formula that kept Doris Day out of Rock Hudson's clutches until the knot was tied.

It is common practice to double the sitcom couple into a foursome. As on "Maude" and "The Ropers," the lead married couple becomes friendly with another couple: the Kramdens with the Nortons, the Rileys with the Gillises, the Ricardos with the Mertzes. On "All in the Family," Gloria and Mike stood in for the other couple, though the Bunkers also had a few sets of neighbors—like the Jeffersons—designed to trigger Archie's Pavlovian prejudices. The two couples can form strong friendships, male to male (Ralph Kramden and Ed Norton) and female to female. Thus, "I Love Lucy" founded two sitcom traditions. From the Lucy/Ricky relationship came all the "I married a dingbat but I love her" series. From the wonderful friendship of Lucy and Ethel Mertz come all the "My Friend Irma," "Rhoda," "Mork," and "Laverne" shows in which loyalty and love prove stronger than reason, and more fun.

Like Lucy and Ethel before them, Laverne and Shirley have charged into one scheme after another. The difference is that Laverne and Shirley are trying to get *ahead,* to make it. Their men are not supporting husbands, only friends. In a way Laverne and Shirley, factory workers, want what Lucy and Ethel have—a married, middle-class life. Their series represents a significant economic shift in sitcoms towards working-class characters; as comedies about lawyers ("Adam's Rib," "The Associates") have become less popular, comedies about blue-collar workers, about waitresses and cab drivers, succeed by taking us back to that most unsuburban world of "The Honeymooners," where the common themes are coping with poverty and working on an American dream to escape it.

But there is also a way in which Lucy and Ethel, happily-married middle-class women of the fifties, wanted what Laverne and Shirley have—the knowledge that they can support themselves, the freedom to define themselves. That Lucy went sneaking behind Ricky's patriarchal back to earn money to replace "his" money, or to try breaking into his show business world; that she dragged Ethel with her (and with Ethel each of us)—all this secret rebellion tells us something about why "I Love Lucy" was America's favorite situation comedy from the very beginning, and why the character Lucy has given birth to so many zany children. "My name is Morky Ricardo," Mork tells the psychiatrist at his sanity hearing. "My best friends are Fred and Ethel Mertz."

24.

Seasons of the Private Eye

Michael Wood

They have a tired look. Their eyes are heavy with the horrors they have seen. Their shrugs, grimaces, wisecracks, indicate a patience and wisdom that cannot be surprised. Yet they are not cynical. They never give up the struggle, and that is why we trust them, why we tune in again and again as they stalk assorted malefactors through hour-long segments of evening or late-night viewing time.

They are television's detectives, private and public: Kojak, Angie Dickinson, Rockford, Karl Malden, Baretta, Jack Klugman, Ironside, Peter Falk, Magnum, Rock Hudson and Susan St. James, Starsky and Hutch, Jonathan Hart and Stephanie Powers. I am lumping together current and canceled programs, as well as reruns, because that is how they appear to many viewers—well, at least to this viewer. Television has an interesting way of tampering with time, of turning dead and living shows into contemporaries.

I have also mixed performers and roles in the above list because I believe that, too, is part of how we perceive these characters. Many of the actors have screen histories. Karl Malden came to "The Streets of San Francisco" from the badlands of *On the Waterfront* and *One-Eyed Jacks*. Jack Klugman's puzzled, dogged "Quincy" is shadowed by his earlier, amiable, disorderly contribution to "The Odd Couple." And they both seem to bring their old problems with them. They have been here before. *Here* is on film, but in a country where the past has become scarce, any sort of history begins to look like a treasure. Think of all those nostalgic 'roasts" now infesting prime time. Celebrities choke themselves on memories, and we weep along. These people remember yesterday, when movies were movies (never mind what the world was like), when men were men and women were June Allyson.

Not all television's detectives are wary and wise. Charlie's Angels, with or without Farah Fawcett, glisten with innocence and hair-softener, and bound into every new scrape with a perfect confidence that their writers cannot fail to rescue them. But the Angels are not *real* detectives—not in the sense that Kojak or Rockford or Columbo are. The pleasures of watching this program have nothing to do with adventure or the trailing of crooks, and everything to do with looking at these radiant, springy, not-quite-human women, pages of *Vogue* shuffled into the semblance of a story. The show has come to fitful life only when one of the Angels has fallen in love—usually with a charming, rugged bad guy, a man who has stepped out of the other half of the fashion plate. The Angels are just romantic heroines in flimsy detective drag, strays in a kingdom of half-hearted crime.

The Harts are another exception—but they *are* real detectives. They win out by wit and charm rather than patience and wisdom—and they never look tired. Their style recalls films like *The Thin Man* or *The Lady Vanishes,* where crime always courted comedy and was a form of mischief rather than menace.

There was until recently a third series, offering an even trickier exception to the rule of weariness. Robert Urich, in "Vega$," is a shrewd, quick, private eye. And he's not tired either. He *is* surprisingly fallible, though. Private eyes are always fallible and vulnerable, but Urich, alias Dan Tana, is vulnerable in not-quite-expected ways. He is not *ritually* wounded like Rockford or Marlowe or Lew Harper, whose bruising and bashing are some sort of ceremonial ordeal. Some of the most delicately shocking moments in recent television years have appeared on "Vega$," and Tana has been as shocked as we were. A strangler is on the loose, for example, and an old girl friend of Tana's is threatened. She is perky, appealing, and we are interested in her—in part because she has resumed her relationship with Tana. In older films and almost all television shows, this interest would be enough to save her life. She would be *nearly* killed: The suspense and the last-minute escape would be part of the package. In this episode of "Vega$" she *is* killed, and Tana, busy, dry-eyed, desperate, mourns throughout the remaining forty minutes or so.

In another episode, a distraught father, lumpy, touching, provincial, asks Tana to find his runaway daughter for him. Tana does, and the father, with the faintest changes of expression and intonation—wince turns to sneer, whine becomes threat—reveals himself as the evil leader of a gang that is after the secrets the girl has stolen. Tana was taken in, and so were we. Only the girl, haunted, terrified (and pregnant for good measure), sees at once what Tana has done. Of course he mends matters before the show is over, and even delivers the baby, but I can't think of another fictional detective who is allowed such a lapse. Sam Spade's slips, Rockford's constant bungling, Philip Marlowe's incessant stumbling into ugly ambushes, offer nothing like the potential for damage *to others* provided by Tana's error.

The single most interesting change in television detectives in recent years is the tremendous increase in the number of policeman-heroes. Tana, Rockford, Marlowe, Harper, Harry O, and a few others are private detectives, while all the rest are policemen (one is a policewoman). Angie Dickinson a cop? The dancing girl who made such sly, irreverent fun of Sheriff John Wayne in *Rio Bravo*? "Police Woman"? The very title would hardly have been thinkable in the fifties and sixties. A new show called "Strike Force" made its appearance and "The FBI," which *was* thinkable in those distant days, returned with a face-lift. Police detectives are nowhere near as vulnerable as private eyes, however ritualized this vulnerability may be; private eyes do not face the political complications—the superiors anxiously requiring premature results—that permanently afflict Kojak, Quincy, McCloud, Starsky and Hutch, and the rest.

We are worlds away from "The Fugitive," and other earlier series, where the hero was an architect or a journalist, a solitary figure deriving no support from a deluded system. We are worlds away too from the tradition of the old private eye, from Sherlock Holmes and the Saint to Marlowe and Harper, who are all impatient with the system, rattled by its delays, or scornful of its lack of imagination. Rockford and Tana, in spite of their differences, belong to this tradition, and that is why their shows feel so nostalgic—Rockford is frankly, agreeably nostalgic, Tana secretly nostalgic, an old-fashioned type who has been attractively but only superficially modernized.

The "public" detective (as distinct from the private kind) may be a new breed of hero on American television, but not all fictional policemen have been flat-footed foils to the brilliant amateur or freelancer. Mr. Bucket in Dicken's *Bleak House,* Wilkie Collins's Sergeant Cuff in *The Moonstone,* Margery Allingham's Inspector Champion, Simenon's Maigret, the heroes of Ed McBain, all testify to another tradition. It remains true, I think, that until recently, especially in America, the independence of the private eye, his *battles* with the police—even if they were only friendly battles of the kind Rockford repeatedly has with his pal Dennis—were an aspect of his virtue, a form of guarantee that the truth he finally discovered would be his truth (and our truth), not a version tailored to the needs of the rich and the powerful.

What is interesting, and encouraging, is that we have not given up our quest for this sort of truth—or at least we haven't given up watching people look for it on television. We have merely placed our bets, or most of our bets, on a different, less isolated hero. To draw the conclusion a little too crudely: We no longer believe, except in fantasy or nostalgia or parody, that the vulnerable, unattached individual can find out what we want to know. Our newer heroes maintain the independence of the old ones (who could be more stubborn, more loyal to his sense of authentic justice, than Quincy or Baretta?), but they do it against the intimate pressures of an entangled professional life. They don't get beaten up by the bad guys (or by the cops); they get scolded or suspended or fired by their bosses, who in turn are being harassed by the mayor or the attorney general.

The rise of the police detective on television has created the need for new gimmicks. Dennis Weaver's McCloud is a Texan in New York—a simple device, but one that works. Columbo is a policeman who makes like a private eye—shuffling gait, downcast look, scruffy raincoat and all. Quincy is a doctor, interrogating not criminals but corpses—or rather interrogating corpses that lead him to criminals. There have, of course, been repetitions. "Eischeid" was not a bad show, but Joe Don Baker did look like a stand-in for Raymond Burr, and the name of the program itself sounded like a painful mispronunciation of "Ironside." The producers of these series, though, have generally sought, and generally found, diversity. Starsky and Hutch are plainclothesmen constantly in fancy dress, hamming it up as carefree playboys on a Caribbean island, or as wealthy, arrogant gamblers penetrating an illicit club. Both David Soul and Paul Michael

Glaser are gifted comedians; the series offers an interesting counterpoint to "Charlie's Angels," the detective show that isn't, and to "Hart to Hart," the show that flirts with sophisticated comedy. "Starsky and Hutch," like "Hart to Hart," *is* a detective show, but it always verges on slapstick: Starsky and Costello, let's say, or Abbott and Hutch. (It is for this reason that I was surprised by all the complaints about the program's violence. It is not violent; it is funny. What violence there is usually concerns *cars*—metal crashing into metal, or into conveniently placed walls. Can it be that we find violence to property more disturbing than violence to people? Or can't we tell the difference?)

The police, then, have an engaging, multifarious image on television. Robert Blake's Baretta looks like a delinquent kid who might run from Kojak on the street. Kojak himself, when he was only Telly Savalas, was invariably a snarling bad guy, the complacent distributor of death and opium. This implies, I think, that there is no variation of style that television's imaginary police force cannot accommodate. Pluralism is the order of the decade.

What are we looking for in these shows? Detective stories—printed, filmed, staged, televised, recounted—are a special taste. Some people loathe them, and some people attend to nothing else. I can speak only of the latter group, those of us who would rather watch "Name of the Game" (time for a rerun?) than any number of games with names or numbers.

We are looking for *style:* fast music, sharp editing, crisp shooting, brisk dialogue. Detective shows are among the things American television does better than any other nation's networks. Comedy and drama, by contrast, are incomparably better on British television, and the big spectacle is better almost anywhere. We are also looking for a reflection of our world: a place of cars, highways, highrises, offices, slums, water coolers, coffee shops, bars, threats, and fear. Crime is always contemporary, even when its tone is nostalgic. The programs put out faint feelers in the direction of the seething social ills that are banished from all the happier shows. Or to say it another way, detective series are the least *stagey* of television shows. Even when they are shot in a studio, they manage to look as if they are full of streets. Above all, it seems to me, we are looking for *reassurance*—which is none the less satisfying because it is imaginary. If it were real, we wouldn't need to look for it on television.

We have our forms of magic. Though we don't believe it will rain just because we enact certain rites, and we don't believe crime will go away just because Jack Klugman or James Garner has tracked a fictitious evildoer to his equally fictitious lair, these shows do present, week after week, remarkable triumphs over difficult odds. We may not be persuaded that delinquency doesn't pay, or that good must win. We *are* persuaded, however, that character is virtue, and that virtue is a mixture of tenacity and good fortune, a matter of hanging on tight until the lucky break occurs.

There is a serious difference between American detective shows (and films and novels) and English or French mystery writing. A mystery is a puzzle, a riddle to be solved by the sleuth and the reader, and its ultimate implication is a promise about the orderliness and intelligibility of the world. Among recent television shows, only "Columbo" makes much of this sort of appeal. All the other detectives are intelligent enough, of course, but their intelligence is not their chief weapon, and neither, finally, is their skill—or even their experience, in any practical sense. Their chief weapon is their stubbornness, their unshakable honesty, in a word, their *character.* They conquer crime in show after show not out of ingenuity or guile, not because of what they know or because of what they can do, but because of *who they are.* Not to imply that the world is orderly in the eyes of gods and detectives; only that decency and persistence can make a dent in the power of those twin nuisances, crooks and officialdom. And this is why television's detectives are so likable, so trustworthy, so tired, and with one or two exceptions, so old. We have to know they won't crack or quit, and that they can count on their luck—that their luck, too, is part of their character.

The reassurance they offer is not a simple affair; magic is never simple. What they propose to us, by the sheer accumulation of their victories, is that honor and endurance really do get us somewhere—even in reality, perhaps. Or if we feel the need for a more skeptical claim, they suggest that honor and endurance can't do us any harm, and are worth remembering in case we ever run into them again. The world is not a better place for these shows, but it is less of an invitation to despair. Virtues that are demonstrated, if only in fiction, are more real than those never mentioned at all; just as named ghosts are less terrifying than unnamed, unnameable abominations.

In this perspective I think we can see the particular interest of "Vega$," and the continuity as well as the change represented by the influx of policemen into television. "Vega$" plays with this reassurance, threatens to take it away, but always restores it. Kate Columbo simply couldn't provide it, and this perhaps was one of the reasons for the short run of the show. She was an ordinary, pleasant woman whose character gave no indication that she was bound to win the fight, and whose vulnerability was just that: awful, terminal vulnerability.

As the sixties faded away, we fell in love with law and order, and the crowds of policemen on television—the fact that they *are* policemen—expressed and continue to express that love. That is obvious enough and dreary enough. But the variety, and independence of mind, and appeal, of most of these policemen, express something older: a sense that the detective, within the system or outside it, is always different, always alone, always a rarity—which makes him valuable to us. Not because he represents some extravagant, ornery old individualism, but because he preserves things we are afraid may be endangered, like decency and tenacity and truth. The detective is not exactly a fantasy or even the fulfillment of a wish. He is more like the disheveled embodiment of a flickering hope.

ica, which nourishes individualism, has nourished some pretty weird individuals. There are the members of a seemingly ordinary California family, who chat amiably about Rebecca, a ghost they've adopted from a spirit adoption agency, or there's the young man who leaps from Milwaukee's Holland Drive Bridge onto the Milwaukee River to water-ski at forty miles an hour *without skis,* or the professor of physics who "risks his life" by driving into four upended cars that crash into flames as he topples them. One wonders why an apparently sane academician would care to spend his time demolishing the products of General Motors in this reckless fashion. Had he once bought a lemon? Is this a symbolic attack on our American obsession with the automobile? There seems to be no explanation except the deep and abiding strain of dottiness pervading our population. These shows seem to be saying that under our polyester, we're a nation of crackpots.

Presiding over this array of unhinged Americana are moderators unblemished by the least smear of eccentricity. In contrast to the "real people" who provide the material of the shows, the hosts are all bland, impeccably well-groomed, and about as magnetic as display-window mannequins. While "That's Incredible!" and "Real People" are similar, each approaches its material in a different way. "That's Incredible!" has a fondness for yogis, stunts, odd coincidence, bizarre medical anomalies, and supernatural phenomena. "Real People," along with its winsome octogenarians, adorable pets, and dippy characters, throws in a bit of patriotism, "feminism," and tongue-in-cheek sociology.

"That's Incredible!" generally opens on a note of derring-do, with some yogi or another deep in hypnotic trance, lying beneath a platform over which a three-ton elephant is about to lumber, or resting his muscled neck on a machete blade while a forty-pound block of concrete is placed on his forehead, or calmly awaiting decapitation while a cutting blade descends, pit-and-pendulum-style, toward his exposed throat. Across the screen flashes the warning, "Don't try this!" (Do they really imagine that across the nation, impressionable high-school boys are rigging up contraptions meant to pulverize human flesh in imitation of superhuman Hindus? Anyway, it's pretty hard to get your hands on a three-ton elephant.) There's a drum roll, a moment of bated breath, then the elephant moves, the blade falls, the sledgehammer demolishes the concrete block, and the yogi emerges—unscathed, of course. This is about as suspenseful as watching a cartoon character plummet from a cliff only to bounce resiliently up again. "That's incredible," the audience announces with a trace of disappointment, as if it would have been more fun to watch the yogi get pulverized before its very eyes.

Another predominant theme of this show is the supernatural. Over several weeks I observed a haunted toy store, a haunted pub, two haunted houses, two UFO sightings, and some Haitian zombies. Fascination with the unexplainable appears to be a current national preoccupation. Professor Theordore Roszak of San Francisco State University commented in a recent issue of *Harper's* that "more and more frequently, I find myself at conferences and gatherings in the company of learned and professional people who are deliberately and unabashedly dabbling in a sort of higher gullibility, an assertive readiness to give all things astonishing, mind-boggling, and outrageous the chance to prove themselves true." Sensing this widespread appetite for the arcane, "That's Incredible!" trots viwers through innumerable haunted premises. "This is a re-creation," captions advise, as candles flicker and otherworldly voices whisper. But these hokey re-creations reduce mystery to banality. Take the segment in which psychic Sylvia Brown is called upon to make contact with the toy-store ghost. A teddy bear mysteriously topples from a shelf. Intruding on this gripping scene is the television crew, cameras loaded with high-speed, infrared film. Sylvia has "picked up" the name of John Johnson, a ghost who periodically roams the aisles in search of his lost love, a lady who once lived on the toy store site. Although John bled to death in an accident more than 200 years ago, Sylvia says he doesn't realize he's dead. To correct this oversight, she admonishes him to "cross to the other side." John obediently departs, leaving nothing behind but his blurred form on the developed photographs.

Another segment concerned Haitian zombies. For those unversed in voodoo practice, zombies are people whose dead bodies ostensibly have been exhumed and injected with a chemical from a flower called a "zombie cucumber." These living dead are then carted off to zombie plantations, where they become the unwilling slaves of voodoo priests. One such victim was François Narcisse, dead and buried eighteen years ago, who recently turned up in his native village after an intervening period of bondage. As proof of his death, we're told, François bears a scar on his cheek where it was pierced by a coffin nail. Because he could read and write, François was promoted to zombie-supervisor, which goes to show that while there may not be sex after death, there's still career advancement. His singular biography is recited in the same matter-of-fact tone characterizing all "That's Incredible!'s" ghostly goings-on. No doubts whatsoever are raised about the veracity of his story, nor are any other possible explanations for his long disappearance proffered. He is simply among us, as commonplace as the postman.

"That's Incredible!," contrary to its own professed intentions, consistently turns the potentially marvelous into the mundane. While heartsick ghosts and escaped zombies may not be entitled to better treatment, a gifted child named Alicia Witt and a priest named Ralph DiOrio of St. John's Church in Worcester, Massachusetts, are. Alicia, a pretty, blond youngster, is representative of children who exhibit signs of outstanding intelligence or talent at an early age. Kids who compose symphonies at ten, or speak four languages while their peers are struggling to master one, are truly remarkable. A television program that took a serious look at this phenomenon would be worth watching. Instead, Alicia is invited into the studio, where she's asked to perform the balcony scene from *Romeo and Juliet* with the show's host. Alicia complies, lisping her lines with stunning incomprehension while the audience coos. Such playacting might seem harmless, but I contend there's something insidious in treating an intelligent child like a gussied-up performing poodle.

I found equally offensive the inclusion of Father DiOrio, a man of seemingly authentic faith, among the show's usual collection of sky-diving amputees, car wreckers, and motorcycle-racing dogs. Father DiOrio performs faith-healing cures at his church services. On two different nights, I watched a cripple walk after years in a wheelchair, a child who was going blind regain her full sight, and a man whose clubfeet were healed by the reverend's touch. To observe people whose abiding faith in God cures them could be a moving experience, but so indifferently is the sacred intermingled with the profane that a miracle becomes just another stunt.

"Real People" rarely offends, but often disappoints by striking upon a topic of considerable interest, and then failing to develop it. Take the segment concerning punks—a fascinating subculture. Punks dancing at New York City's Mudd Club were labeled "wacky, tacky street urchins." Some culinary delectables were exhibited: "Chicken on a Clothesline" (several scrawny birds strangled and strung up), "Baby in Jello" (a dismembered rubber doll in a gelatin mold). The punks fell upon this revolting fare and gobbled it up while the sound track snorted and chortled with glee. It *was* funny, but are the punks really "wacky, tacky kids" or an angry, alienated element of our society? Whizzing to the next bit, "Real People" doesn't pause to ask or answer such questions.

Despite this criticism, I found appealing the show's choice of feisty, outrageous characters. Among my favorites was Alan J. Weberman, a man whose mission in life is to rummage through celebrity garbage. Weberman rifled Bob Dylan's trash cans for years, and has now cast a wider net, which includes Norman Mailer (several betting slips), Gloria Vanderbilt (an empty Valium bottle), David Rockefelller (a letter to the Duke of York with the salutation "Dear Dukie"), Jackie Onassis (torn panty hose), and Richard Nixon (Bebe Rebozo's unlisted telephone number).

"Real People" also has a predilection for sexy octogenarians. One standout in this category is Disco Sally, who has spent her twilight years shaking her booty at Studio 54 and other Manhattan hot spots. Sally recently wed a good-looking Greek and plans to get it on with him at least once or twice before she passes on. (No doubt, after her demise, she'll reappear on "That's Incredible!" as the Disco Ghost). Another charmer is eighty-year-old Leo Ledelman, who practices his violin for two hours daily in a public restroom in Los Angeles. Leo plucks and bows with evident zest, oblivious of the bemused stares of those using the restroom for more down-to-earth purposes. His romantic life is equally unconventional. Leo has a twenty-five-year-old girlfriend he picked up at a bus stop. Music and sex light up his life. As an antidote to the ravages of old age, who wouldn't choose music and sex over prune juice and Geritol?

But perhaps the single most irritating feature of the show is a penchant for the corniest jokes this side of a seventh-grade classroom. Example: "I hear you got in the ring last week with a pair of wrestlers." "Yes, and it was a very touching experience." Everyone, from hosts to audience, engages in the kind of moldy badinage that makes one wince. This hee-haw humor serves to dull the cutting edge of sly satire informing many of the segments, and detracts from the uninhibited and genuinely funny personalities of the show's multifarious screwballs.

Since I could not unearth a single adult among my friends or colleagues who watched any of these programs, I wondered who else, besides myself, was tuned in. According to network figures,

"Real People" and "That's Incredible!" draw between 30 million and 40 million viewers each for an average episode. Since my teenage sons and several of my high school English students were the only ones with whom I could discuss the mystifying matter of spontaneous human combustion, I concluded that the audience was predominantly adolescent. It turns out that "Real People's" viewers are mostly adults of both sexes (only a measly 7 percent of its audience are teens). During the football season, the bulk of "That's Incredible!'s" fans are males, since it goes on before or after football. This would explain why "That's Incredible!" is more fixated on stunts, acts of athletic daring, and other exhibitions of macho preening.

Although they take their material from "real life," these shows are far from realistic. Horace Newcomb, professor of English at the University of Texas and writer of numerous articles on television, believes the appeal of a show like "That's Incredible!" may be attributed to an abiding human interest in the bizarre, the spectacular, and the strange. "Everybody likes to go to a sideshow," he explains. "Leslie Fiedler's book about freaks documents this need to look at the unseemly. As a child, I always read "Ripley's Believe It or Not" in the newspapers, and my sons buy the *Guinness Book of World Records*. Whether or not a show about *real* people would ever be successful is another matter."

According to its executive producer, George Schlatter, "Real People" does not satisfy a craving for the grotesque in the American public but a need for affirmation. Schlatter feels his show struck a responsive chord in a country guilty over its role in Vietnam, horrified by its declining economy, and troubled by its ecological headaches. "The timing was right," he points out. "Americans wanted to feel good, to be proud. We wanted a sense of accomplishment. 'Real People' isn't just concerned with eccentrics, but with role models and heroes. Each show presents a hero or someone who has done something worthwhile. Our show celebrates the American individual, which is a departure. Unlike the English, we tend to hide our individuals, while they cherish theirs." Schlatter feels his show has had the greatest impact, not on imitations, but on the news. Sensing that the public is fed up with murder and rape, news programs ape entertainment shows by offering "eight minutes of news, interspersed with chitchat, banter, and a real-people story. It's show biz." As Horace Newcomb speculates, the news might be our *real* real-people show.

Well, maybe. But the news still does not treat unexceptional people living unexceptional lives—nor, in fact, does television in general. Even Frederick Wiseman's documentaries, whose subjects are mental patients and welfare clients, only examine life at society's fringe. The point is sometimes made that ordinary people are too boring to hold an audience's attention, but "An American Family," the PBS documentary series in 1973, proved this false. Far from dull, the saga of the William C. Loud family was a compelling, if sometimes too painful, exposure of one family's daily life. Real people are not dreary, but we've yet to find television's equivalent of Studs Terkel: someone willing to allow real people to reveal themselves on camera without artifice.